When Love Wins

Our Journey to Peace

―――――――

Tami L. Hawley

Enjoy the journey!

Tami L Hawley

When Love Wins: Our Journey to Peace
Copyright © 2014 by The Divine Dove
(www.TheDivineDove.com)

All rights reserved. No part of this book may be reproduced or transmitted in any form or by any means without written permission from the author.

ISBN (9780991505807)

Cover design by tlhawley and malee
Printed in USA by 48HrBooks (www.48HrBooks.com)

Dedication

To my mother, Arlene......

You always made me shine
And stand up on my own.
And all those times you stood next to me.
You always let me fly
And soar against the wind.
And all those times you flew next to me.
You always let me dream
And walk above the clouds.
And all those times you kept me on the ground.
You always let me try
And learn with every fall.
And all those times you caught me on the way.
You are the wings that lifted me.
You are the wind I needed to fly.
You are the love that saved me.

And to my husband, Bob....

MTTY LTT

Foreword

"I'm going to show you a peace so beautiful you'll probably forget what your life has been like up until now."
– Joan Brady, *God on a Harley*

It began with *God on a Harley*. A colleague recommended Joan Brady's book to me when we were away at a business conference. She saw how unhappy and depressed I was, counseled me and told me I was worthy.

I read the book twice. I'd encountered books like this before but I think timing was everything. I'd gone through a divorce, lost my identity, never became what and who I wanted to be, and felt my entire twenties had been wasted. Carol, and that book, came into my life at the right time and changed my life. At that moment, I decided Carol was right – I *was* worthy. I, like everyone else, deserved to be happy and loved.

I'd searched before, but that moment set me on a deeper spiritual journey of discovery. It's been a long path with twists and turns, yields and stop signs, and even some pretty big potholes. But I wouldn't trade any of it because of the lessons I have learned.

After deciding it was time to pick myself back up, I went to a psychic healer who was also my counselor. Nancie recommended a book called *Let Your Life Speak* by Parker J. Palmer. I read the book and highlighted all the passages that rang true to me. This past year I picked that book up again. Everything I highlighted back then I was beyond now. I was grateful I had come so far. I highlighted new paragraphs and words and phrases and suddenly, what I had been looking for, my life's purpose, was clear. I'd been an avid reader and writer my entire life. Spirituality was something I'd always felt so deeply. Maybe now was the time to combine all my passions.

So this project started. I wondered if I could help others by showing how I took the lessons I learned and applied them to my life. Maybe there was an easier way for people to "get it" – our reason for being here – without preaching or scaring them off by using words like "religion" and "God." Maybe there was a way to teach this so people would feel a part *of* each other, not apart *from* each other. This book is as much therapy for me as it is guidance for anyone who reads it. Hopefully it will at least make even one person think more, love more.

You have to want to do this and you have to have the right attitude towards it. And most importantly, you have to practice, just like with anything else, in order to turn the lessons into habit. I continue to learn every day. Enlightenment, as it's been defined for us, is rare. Most of us will never reach the levels that Buddha or Mother Theresa or Jesus did. But we can certainly live a much more peaceful life filled with happiness and love. Instead of enlightenment maybe the goal should simply be awareness.

There are some people who emotionally and spiritually won't be ready for the kinds of changes in their life I will talk about. There are some people who refuse to look in the mirror and see how they are responsible for themselves and everything that happens to them. They can't see that what they give out, they get back. There are some people who don't want to look at others with love – they want to find fault in others so they don't have to acknowledge any fault in themselves. I can't fathom why anyone would want to live this way, with constant drama and angst. But then, they don't even see the drama or the angst. They just see it as normal.

I, for one, want more than that. I want a simple life filled with love and happiness and peace. And, after many years of searching and researching, I've realized you aren't going to get that kind of life without looking for it and finally choosing it for yourself.

Introduction

*"The journey of a thousand miles
begins with one step."
– Lao Tzu*

Love. It begins our journey, it ends our journey, and is the foundation for everything we encounter along the way. After all, love is the only thing that is eternal. It is all we need to gain the peace we were all created to experience.

Love will take away the need for forgiveness. Love will conquer negative thoughts such as anger, depression, fear, and jealousy. Love will give us the quiet strength to calm our minds, fill our souls, and help us live a peaceful life. Love will change hope into knowing.

It really is that simple.

This is a spiritual book, not a religious one. Whether you believe in God, Buddha, Allah, or the power within; whether you label yourself Christian, Buddhist, Muslim, or you wear no label, we are all looking for the same thing. We are all looking for peace.

In the following chapters, we will journey through negativity and come out the other side. Get a journal; even buy yourself a nice new pen. Take notes, do the exercises I suggest. Make this a priority in your life. Together we will learn to love and trust ourselves. We will listen, become aware, and appreciate this life. We will realize our life's purpose. We will create miracles.

And we will do all of this together, using love as both our anchor and our wings. Let's begin...

I Am Created Out of Love to Love and Be Loved

"There is a theory which states that if ever anyone discovers exactly what the Universe is for and why it is here, it will instantly disappear and be replaced by something even more bizarre and inexplicable. There is another theory which states this has already happened."
– Douglas Adams, *The Restaurant at the End of the Universe*

I will not pretend to be a scientist of any kind. I will not get into any debate on what you should believe about how we came to be. Whether you believe we evolved from the Big Bang, by either spiritual or scientific forces, or whether you believe that God or a Divine Being created us, or whether you believe a little of both to be true, it is safe to say we were *created*.

Regardless, our creation was an act of love, whether from God, the Divine Mother, Mother Nature, the Source. Even the simple act of evolving – organisms developing, living unobstructed, naturally becoming something out of nothing – is an act of love. In fact, can you get more loving than the simple gesture of being left alone to evolve?

So, we can say we were created out of love. If we were created out of love, all we were created to *know* is love, so all we were created to *do* is love. We were created out of love to love and be loved. It's as simple as that.

Anything else, any other mess we have gotten ourselves into, is our own doing.

Once we realize we were created out of love, it's much easier to see how everything is connected. Not just all humans, all animals – all *creat*ures – but even inanimate objects, objects we think exist without life. Think about the computer you are using, the table it rests upon. Think about the hands that made the machines that may have been used to put that computer together; the hands that sawed the lumber for that table or the hands that cut the tree down. Every*thing* is created by love by some*one* who was created by love. That someone is just like you – they have a name, a body, thoughts, dreams, physical and emotional ailments. They went to work to create something that you are now using, probably taking for granted that it even exists.

Every single thing has life – energy – inside of it. Some people even think that our emotional energy goes into everything we create and everything we do. Think about that as you type your next email, prepare your next meal, kiss your child goodnight. As you communicate and remember that you were created to simply love, are you expressing that sentiment? Or are you expressing anger, gossip, arrogance, impatience, and jealousy? Do you want to spread negative energy or do you want to spread love, happiness, and peace? Does seeing everything and everyone in the world connected this way make you appreciate everything and everyone a little bit more? It should. It's why we're here.

Jesus (historically and spiritually) said if you want to know about life and how to live it just look at a flower. Think about this. First we start with a seed. Where does the seed come from? Oh sure, we can say it comes from the last flower that died and left its seeds behind. But what did *that* flower seed from? We don't often think about this, we take that seed and its existence for granted. We just assume there *is* a seed, we don't think which came first the seed or the flower, and we are content with this.

But isn't this a miracle? Isn't the existence of this tiny little seed the most important part of the entire process? Do we need to understand how this seed came to be before we can appreciate what it will become? Or can we simply acknowledge its existence and allow the seed to take root?

Once the seed takes root it continues to grow, develops a stem and leaves, and then the fruit of its labor begins to bud. It has already gone through so much to get to this stage where we can finally see the beauty of the flower. What kind of flower will it be? What will it look like? What will its characteristics be? What will its purpose be? Does any of that even matter, or can we just appreciate the timeless beauty of the process?

After the flower matures it begins to wilt, decay, lose its color and beauty. Does the miracle cease to exist? Of course not.

The miracle wasn't the evolution or the growth or any enlightenment that took place. The miracle, after all, was in the seed.

Who are you? A miracle. When we take away being defined by what we look like, what we have, what we think, and what we feel, what is left? Love is left. This is who we really are. This is why we were created. This is what we need to journey back to if we wish to find peace.

Repeat this mantra:
I am created *out* of love to love and *be* loved.

I Choose Love

"For love is immortality."
– Emily Dickinson

Love, simply, is. Love is constant, love doesn't change. You can choose to *not* love, but love will still exist. Love is the base – the foundation – of everything. We just have to remember that it is always a matter of choice.

Bring to mind all that you love. Most of us will immediately think of a person. We love our spouses or partners – remember your first kiss, holding hands, waking up next to him in the morning. We love our children – remember the first time you saw her, held her in your arms, watched her take her first step. We love our best friend – remember your first concert with him, laughing uncontrollably at nothing, watching him get married. We love our mother or father – remember how she was at every football game you played in, how he taught you to drive, how proud she was of you at your graduation.

We also love our pets who love us unconditionally and make our house a home. We love how they know their name, how they cuddle next to us on the couch, how they greet us at the door every time we return home.

We love the feel of sunshine on our faces, the sound of rain against the roof at night, the beauty of winter's first snow. We love the smell of our favorite flowers or warm cinnamon buns baking in the oven; the majesty of the ocean, forest, or mountains; the taste of morning's first cup of coffee or tea. We love our gardens and how nourished we feel after a day surrounding ourselves in their vibrant beauty. We love the feelings and emotions we get from dancing, listening to music, laughing.

Now imagine a world without love. Take all of those things we love and put them away where we can never call them back. It is a dark, destructive, lonely place, isn't it?

Love is everything. Love is all we are. Love is the only thing that really *is*. It's not about who has the most money or the biggest house or the most toys. It's not about being thin or looking young. It's about love. It's about all those things we love and all those things that make us feel loved.

We were created out of love in order to love and be loved. Nothing more, nothing less. Make it more and we get less. If we want love, we need to give love. Because when we give love we will get love back. Guaranteed.

Who are your favorite people? What are your favorite things? Nature, animals, music, dance? Why do you love them? What words would you use about how they make you feel?

"The first kiss from my husband made me feel beautiful."

"The first time I laid eyes on my daughter, I felt blessed."

"When my best friend and I are laughing, I feel undeniable happiness."

"Thinking about everything my mother has done for me makes me feel appreciated and important."

"When my cat curls up next to me, I feel joy."

"Being in nature makes me feel warm, calm, in awe, invincible, alive, peaceful, happy."

What if those words were being used to describe *you*? Wouldn't that be wonderful! When someone speaks of you would you want them to use words like "driven," "wealthy," and "successful?" Or would you rather them use words like "inspiring," "kind," and "happy?" Although the first set of words is by no means bad, which would have a more lasting impression on you? Which person would you want to remember?

What if we could feel that love all the time, or even just most of the time? What if someone told us that we could train ourselves to think differently? What if, at any moment, during any trial, we could call on love? Well, we can.

I'm sure you've heard the phrase "Change your mind, change your life." It's not spiritual mumbo-jumbo. If you commit to it, it really does work. Everything is in your mind. So instead of choosing anger, jealousy, and guilt, why not choose love?

Love is a choice. How you choose to go about your day and react to each person and situation is up to you.

Life is stressful. Work that consumes more than just our time spent in the office; responsibilities that fill all of our "free" time; friends and family we feel constant demands from; news we have access to at all times from unlimited sources – our fast-paced lives are filled with negative energy. We go and go and go and our thoughts spin out of control until we are tired and sick.

How much of what you do every day is really something that defines you? How often do you allow yourself to retreat to what makes you smile and brings you joy? Does the stress outweigh the peace and love you could have instead? Do you think about work constantly? Do you dread talking to your friend because you just can't hear one more "awful" thing that's happened to her today? Do you sometimes wish you could just get in your car and drive and not look back?

You don't have to quit your job or lose your friends or fall into solitude to live a life of love. You can choose to go through your day with a smile on your face instead of a frown. You can choose to fulfill your obligations and responsibilities with a light heart instead of a heavy one. You can choose to be the person you are meant to be instead of the person you have become, always feeling like life has dealt you a bad hand. If you change your mind to choose love instead of stress, maybe that great new job will find you. Maybe you will bring people into your life who believe in you. Maybe you will start believing in yourself.

Choose love and love will find you. Decide what is more important. Would you rather have peace of mind or be right? Would you rather love or hate? Would you rather feel whole again or continue to play the victim? If you said the latter in each of these then this book isn't for you. It's for the rest of us who have decided we've had enough. It's for the rest of us who have decided happiness is more important than anything egotistical or materialistic. It's for the rest of us who want peace.

How do we start choosing love? Well, to begin with, we will never hear ourselves think or use words like "stupid," "idiot," "ugly," and "lazy," when talking about ourselves *or* anyone else. Instead we use words like "smart," "funny," "beautiful," and "nice." When choosing love we will not feel depressed, angry, hopeless, and afraid. We will feel content, happy, calm, and peaceful. And if we can't find a way to feel these things, then we choose to let the negativity go, and those positive feelings will find us. Have a negative thought, push it aside. Can't seem to find love? Walk away.

When you always choose love, you always get absolute truth. That truth may not always be the outcome you expected, or even wanted, but it will be the right one if you desire peace. Maybe you realize to obtain peace you have to leave your job or dissolve a relationship. If you were truthful, if you chose love instead of negativity in trying to work through the angst, those endings will always bring you new and better beginnings. When you can honestly say you've chosen love at least most of the time – if not every time – you will then know beyond a doubt when to continue the battle or when to walk away; when to let your child do something or when to let them hate you for a little while because you know what's best for them; when to stay in your marriage or when to leave.

If you walk away without the truth of always choosing love – you have held on to anger, continue to argue and blame, never take any responsibility of your own – you will continue to invite nothing but negativity into your life. You will always find destructive relationships; you will hate every job you take; and your children will be spoiled, feel entitled, and continue to walk all over you. These negative patterns will repeat until you've learned your lesson and learned what choosing love means. Only love can put a stop to the hurt and finally heal you and your life.

What has happened in the past to hurt you and stain your heart? Is there a present situation that mirrors that? You have been given another opportunity to do it right. Was your prior relationship physically abusive, or did your partner abuse drugs or alcohol? Does your partner work too many hours or hang out with his friends more than you would like? Does your current husband have a similar issue? Maybe he's addicted to video games or television. Maybe he would rather spend his spare time watching sports or surfing the internet than share time with you.

Are you responding the same way this time that you did last time? Are you continuing to wait around for him to finally choose you to spend his time with? Are you telling him his addictions are *his* problem and not doing anything to help him and support him through his healing? If you are continuing the pattern, you will get the same result – unhappiness. Whether you end up divorced a second time or decide to stay in a bad marriage, you choose that unhappiness by not choosing love.

You will continue to attract the same people or incidents into your life until you learn what you are supposed to from them. If there is a struggle in your life, ask yourself what you are supposed to learn from it. Is it patience or humility? Is your lesson that you seem to be able to extend compassion to your friends but when it comes to your spouse or children you can't? Change your mind, change your life. Look inside yourself for the answer instead of blaming someone – or something – else, and you will find the love and peace that have been eluding you.

Choosing love changes everything. How could it not when love *is* everything? Choose love. The more you do, the more love will also choose you. It will change your life and maybe even help change the life of someone else along the way. That is the miracle choosing love will create.

Repeat this mantra all day today:
I choose love.

I Am Love

"You cannot be lonely
if you like the person you're alone with."
– Wayne Dyer

Give love and you will get love. We must learn to accept and love others. But first we must learn to accept and love ourselves. We tend to define ourselves by our physical body and by what others' opinions of us are. We think we know our self. But we don't. The only way to truly know our self is by looking within. If we want to be happy, we need to be happy. If we want to be alone, we should be alone. If we want to be loved, we need to love.

It starts by looking in the mirror.

Ask yourself, "Do I like what I see?" Write down whatever words come to mind as you look at yourself. How do they make you feel? Most of us will use unloving words like fat, short, or old; negative words that make us feel hurt, angry, and unloved. Now take all those negative words you just wrote down and throw them away. Never use them again.

Look at yourself in the mirror again, this time with love. Use only positive, affirming words like healthy, proportioned, and beautiful. Realize who you are looking at is only a body – a body just like everyone else; a body unlike any other being or thing; a body that proves how alike we human beings are; a body that shows we are all the same.

Close your eyes. Tell yourself who you are. Do not use unloving words like depressed, lonely, or lost. Use only positive, affirming words like smart, independent, and alive. This is who matters. This is who you should be looking at. This is who you want the world to see. This is who you want everyone to know. And this is who everyone wants you to see in them.

List all the non-physical qualities you admire or like in other people: a good sense of humor, a strong work ethic, compassion, kindness, honesty, a loving personality. Don't *you* have a good sense of humor? Can't you think of one time you made someone else laugh? Aren't you compassionate, kind, honest, loving? Can't you think of one time you showed compassion and kindness? Haven't you been honest and loving at least once?

Maybe you realize you admire a quality like a strong work ethic in someone else but you don't share that attribute. Change it. Choose differently. Choose to love yourself enough – that funny, compassionate, kind, honest, loving self – to be on time for work today, to work honestly without excuses, to not call in sick when you aren't. Now you have a good work ethic today. And tomorrow you choose the same. Wednesday comes and you realize you're surfing the internet instead of doing what you are supposed to be doing or instead of maybe volunteering to help a co-worker finish their task. Guess what? You became aware of it and can make the choice to go back to having a good work ethic. You can change that moment and choose love. You just created a miracle.

Take today and notice the times you are hard on yourself, even write them down. What was I doing, why did I not treat myself with love, what emotion do I feel towards myself right now? Once you become aware of the negative feelings or emotions that arise, love yourself and let them go.

Your wrinkles become laugh lines. Your gray hairs become life experiences. Your jeans fitting a little bit tighter remind you of the delicious chocolate ice cream you had for dessert last night.

"I have gained so much weight."

"I have so much work to do."

"I don't have the money to donate to that fundraiser."

As you become aware of each of these negative statements let them go just as quickly, and love and accept yourself at that moment. If a friend says, "I have gained so much weight," how would you respond? Most likely with, "No! You're beautiful!" Respond to yourself the same way. Be kind; treat yourself the way you want to be treated. Love yourself the way you want to be loved – with true acceptance. See yourself differently; see yourself with love.

"I love the way this shirt looks on me."

"I will organize and work efficiently today."

"It is wonderful to see how many people are being so generous."

Change your mind. It takes practice just like any other skill; you need to repeat it until you have made it a habit. That's how you made all of your bad habits, by doing them over and over again. Now choose to make good habits, continuing to give *them* life instead.

"I'll never get a book published" will change to "I'm going to write today."

"I'll never get that promotion" will change to "I am proud of my strong work ethic and desire for self-satisfaction."

"I will never find a partner" will change to "I attract love in all forms because love is what I give."

When I was a little girl, I loved the fairy tale of Cinderella. A beautiful girl in a beautiful dress and beautiful glass slippers being taken out of her awful home by a wonderful and dashing Prince Charming. I wanted to be Cinderella. I by no means had an awful home. And I certainly never wore beautiful dresses and glass slippers (except for my first wedding, where I wore both). But being rescued by Prince Charming? That was my dream. Every woman in my immediate family had been divorced and I was determined to be the one to change all of that. I was the one who would find a man, keep a man, have my own house, never be abused physically or verbally, never be cheated on. I would be happy because I would have this man and that house.

I never wanted a boyfriend in high school or college; at least that's what I told myself. Of course I did. I thought by saying I didn't want one, I wouldn't want one. I wouldn't be sad that I wasn't asked to either of my proms, that I never got asked out on dates, that someone would like me for only a few hidden moments and never talk to me again afterwards. For a long time I never thought it was about me loving them – I thought it was about them loving me. The few boys who said they liked me I didn't believe, so I never gave them the time of day or I ended up hurting them in the end. No one I liked ever liked me back so how could they possibly like me?

So the first man who decided to be with me who I liked first and stayed, I married. I was thirty. We'd been together for nine years, a relationship that after three years I knew wasn't right for me. At that point I had already allowed my self-esteem to fall so low that I believed what I was looking for didn't exist, that my idea of what a marriage was supposed to be was, well, a fairy tale. So I stayed with the wrong man.

My marriage ended after two short years and I suffered a depression that stemmed from deep self-loathing. I wasn't angry at my ex-husband or even at the fact that the relationship after eleven years was over. I was angry at myself for the choices I'd made concerning boys and men my entire life. I was angry that I'd let my twenties go by without once asking myself if I was happy, if I was fulfilling any of my dreams outside of the relationship. I had left the only job I thought I'd have, I was no longer happy in any job I took, and I looked and felt terrible. I let all that time pass not realizing that not only did I lose who I used to be, in all of my adult life I don't think I ever really knew who I was at all.

Over the next few years I did a lot of soul-searching. Many things I did and continue to do are included throughout these pages. Maybe they will help you find something you too have lost. But during those years I also realized that my idea of Cinderella was all wrong; I'd missed the point altogether.

It wasn't about the dress, the shoes, the castle, even being rescued by the prince. It was the fact that – whether cleaning the cinders from the fireplace, waiting on her stepmother and stepsisters, dressing up in fancy clothes for a glorious ball and then losing all of it at midnight – Cinderella was the same girl the entire time. She made no excuses for who she was, she just *was*. She loved and accepted herself no matter what the circumstance. And Prince Charming loved her. Her. Not her hair, her makeup, her gown, even her shoes. He loved *her*. She accepted her circumstances without complaint, lived her dreams and was true to herself despite what others thought or told her, and the love she showed herself was reflected back to her. She created her own miracles.

We become unnaturally attached to material possessions and people because we believe they symbolize our own self-worth. We are dull and unlikeable without that man or woman or these things. We even develop unhealthy addictions that lead us to wanting and needing more because we feel worthless.

We cannot expect others to fulfill our dreams for us or even to make us happy. We cannot expect "things" to fill emotional voids. We cannot expect a pill or a doctor alone to cure us of our physical and mental ailments. We cannot expect to just wake up one day a better, stronger, richer, happier person without exerting any effort of our own.

Only you can know the absolute true nature about yourself beyond the person you display to the world. People or things cannot give you value or worth. You have and are those things already.

Make a list of the people and tangible things in your life that make you happy. Or if you feel you have nothing, make a list of people and things you think you need in your life to make you happy. Perhaps on that list is a spouse or partner, better friends, a bigger house, a higher social status, a better career, children. Observe yourself through these things, or think about why you think your life would be better because of them.

Now ask yourself if you are a better person because of them. Are you better because you have or would have a spouse or partner? Are you able to be loved more because your house is now bigger? Are you able to love yourself and others more simply because you now have children? No, you are still you with the same love inside.

Love does not change because of who or what is in it. We are still important, loving, caring, honest, compassionate, and kind regardless. We need to love ourselves, and be true to ourselves, by seeing our own worth and value through the eyes of love. I promise, when you begin to see yourself this way, you will watch miracles happen.

What do you love? A pet? Spend time with your pet. Notice the unconditional love you give her and that she gives you back. How content are you to just be together? How much love can you feel just playing in the yard or sitting on the couch? Notice how your pet looks at you. How happy do you feel that your pet loves you without reservations? Did your pet notice what size clothes you wear? Did she notice you didn't have makeup on or that your hair wasn't perfect? Did she care that you had a bad day at work? Did she ask you for anything other than love and attention?

Do you love your garden? Go admire it. Notice the care you have given it. Notice how it responds to you. How content are you to water and weed it? How proud do you feel that you gave it life and that it relies on you for its beauty? Did your garden notice what size clothes you wear? Did it notice you didn't have makeup on or that your hair wasn't perfect? Did it care that you had a bad day at work? Did you give it anything other than love and attention?

Isn't it easier to simply love unconditionally, without care for appearance or negativity? Isn't it easier to simply show love and attention to whom and what you love? Love yourself this way. Take the time to love yourself the same way you love your pet or your garden.

Simply accept your beauty. Give yourself attention. Love yourself unconditionally.

You are not the perfect body. You are not that big house, the expensive car, the perfect lawn, that high-paying career. You are beyond all of that. See yourself with so much love that you can't help but reflect it out to the world.

Repeat this mantra all day today:
I am love.

I Love Everyone and Everything

"Kindness makes for much better teamwork."
– John Wooden

Maybe you're tired of people. Maybe people make you angry. Maybe you'd rather live on top of a mountain away from everyone. But here's the thing: we need people. We need each other. We may think we want to be alone but that only gives strength and validation to our loneliness. Letting people in, even just one person, opens our heart to love. And once we do that, our loneliness, our anger, and our fear start to go away.

When we choose love we learn to accept each person as if we are looking at ourselves. We realize everyone is on the same journey; we just walk very different paths. Some paths are long, some are short; some have no obstacles, some have many. But the destination for everyone is the same, and that destination is peace.

In order to find peace, we love and accept ourselves in order to learn how to love and accept others. My friend Priscilla describes it as becoming a multi-faceted crystal that reflects love out in every direction. We should not become sponges that absorb love just to keep it for ourselves. Choosing love means loving others and the world so much that every person feels like family and every place feels like home.

Think about that crystal. When you pour light into it that crystal reflects in every direction, illuminating every inch of space. You are that crystal and how you choose to light your world is what reflects back to you. How you see others will always be a reflection of you, not of them.

How can I be sure that everyone is deserving of love? Because I've done bad things too. I've lied – to others and myself. I've not always been honest. I've made poor choices. I've abandoned – even after being abandoned myself. I've hated instead of loved. But I know I'm not a bad person. I know others would say I am not a bad person. You're not a bad person either. And neither is your neighbor, your co-worker, or your enemy.

What are your judgments saying about you? Sure, there are things we don't know about each other. But what does it matter? You would not let anyone define who you are so do not think for a second you have a right to define anyone else.

Accepting everyone unconditionally sounds impossible, but with practice it won't be. My favorite definition of "acceptance" comes from thesaurus.com – "belief in (the) goodness of something." Believe that everyone has goodness in them. See only the goodness in them. You will be able to accept everyone unconditionally.

Perception is an awful thing made by the ego. It has given us words like "adequate" and "inadequate," "perfect" and "imperfect." It has given us the unnatural idea that we are all different. We definitely all look different. Some of us are slender, some curvy. Some of us are blonde, some brunette. Some of us are short, some tall. Most twins can even be told apart if only by close family and friends. We certainly have different minds, likes and dislikes, thoughts, feelings, dreams. All of this leads us to separation and makes us feel alone in the world with unique problems. No one can possibly understand us, right?

But think how alike we are. We *all* have hopes and dreams. We all have emotions and physical ailments. We all are physically born and we all physically die. We are all looking for happiness, peace, and love. Everyone, no matter how differently they may look at the world, is on the same path.

You can't imagine how amazing you will feel when you start acknowledging that each and every person you encounter is no different than you are. It really isn't as hard as it seems. At least it doesn't have to be. It can be as easy as choosing to see your neighbor as yourself.

Someone told a lie to cover up an error and it infuriates you. Before you cast the first stone think to yourself, "Have I never lied?" Think how you are judging this person and ask yourself if you want to be judged that same way.

Someone told a lie to look better in the eyes of their boss or coworkers. Before you judge them think to yourself, "Have I never told a lie to look better in the eyes of someone else?" Of course you have, we all have.

Instead of judging them for something you too have done, let it go.

What if you were fired or laid off from your job? Your life has been turned upside down. What can you learn? Did you even like this job? Did you try your hardest but just couldn't seem to succeed? Was there something in your life you lost focus of because of this job? Choosing love means accepting this unfortunate event, learning from it, and moving on. Maybe you and your spouse grew apart and now you can mend that relationship. Maybe your wallet was so full you thought you needed more and more to be happy. Learn the lesson that losing this job was meant to teach you. Take the time to reinvent yourself and find a job better suited for you. Perhaps you will need to downsize your life, unclutter unnecessary accumulations, until you find your next job. But see this ending as a new beginning. Choose love and create miracles.

We all know about gossip whether from the office busy-body or the tabloid magazines and television shows we are exposed to. This person is having marriage troubles, that person drinks too much, this person takes twenty smoke breaks during their shift, that person is on the internet all day. Ask yourself if you are always doing an honest day's work. Have you never had an argument in a relationship? Have you never overindulged or dealt with an addiction, whether alcohol, drugs, food, cigarettes? Have you never used your work computer for a single personal thing?

If you gossip, think about someone saying that same thing about you, spreading that same news, those same rumors. Would you want everyone to know about your husband's intimacy problem? Would you want everyone to know about the abortion you had as a teenager? Would you want everyone to know about your child being hauled off to jail? Would you say gossip is a loving gesture? Spreading gossip and starting rumors is not loving. Choosing love means staying silent and letting the moment of judgment pass.

If you have a negative thought, change it to positive. If you can't find a positive thought, stay quiet and let it go.

Take today to notice how often you do not find acceptance in someone or something. Why did you not show love? Write down your findings. By the end of the day you may be surprised at how often you do not choose love. Do not get mad at yourself. Congratulate yourself on becoming aware and decide to be more loving and accepting tomorrow. And keep choosing love until love finally chooses you.

Accept everyone as if looking in the mirror. Believe that everyone has in them the same goodness you see in yourself. Believe that if you see the goodness in everyone they will see the goodness in you. Acceptance will be reflected back to you. Choose one person, maybe the person you see the most at work or the co-worker who gets on your last nerve. Tell yourself, "Today I am going to treat so-and-so with acceptance and love." When this person says something to irritate you, let it pass. If you feel your blood starting to boil, give that feeling away. Let it pass. Write down what you are feeling and then throw the paper out, get up and walk around your office – do whatever you need to do to get rid of the negativity.

Jealousy often keeps us from being able to love and accept others. But life isn't a competition. We were not created to see who can buy the biggest house or have the best friends or make the most money. We were not created to see who can overcome tragedy or who can keep tragedy from entering their lives. We were created simply to love.

"I wish I was as pretty as she is."
"I wish I was as smart as he is."
"I wish my spouse was as great as hers is."
"I wish I made the kind of money he does."
"I wish I could take the kind of vacations they do."

No matter how much we have, we need more because someone we know has something we want or think we can never have. We even measure our own personal strength, our self-worth, on whether our bad stuff is worse than our friends' bad stuff. We want to one-up everyone even with our pain. We can't comment or answer a question without drawing attention to ourselves and our pain or shortcomings.

"I had an abortion."
"Yeah? I gave a child up for adoption."

"I am fighting with my sibling."
"Yeah? I was adopted, I don't have any siblings."

"I am so angry at my child."
"Yeah? I wasn't able to have any children."

I have always been an avid sports fan and have the utmost respect for athletes. Everyone is working together towards the same goal. One person's strength is another's weakness. Limitations aren't important when they are all in it together. Michael Phelps is the premiere swimmer in the history of the summer Olympics. Even in this individualized sport how many other athletes does he make work harder? How many other athletes does he push into personal bests because of how superior he is? There is no reason for envy. His strength helps others focus on making their weaknesses strong and their own strengths even stronger.

What I love about sporting events like the Olympics is that these individual athletes from swimming, track & field, gymnastics, and more are competing for themselves. But they are also competing with their peers in team competitions and for their countries. They are bettering themselves while also contributing to better their teammates. I love when rival athletes hug after an event. "Thank you for pushing me. Thank you for making me stronger." If there is any jealousy there, these athletes still choose love over envy. Without each other they might not be where and who they are today.

Choose to be the example of strength. Choose to show others how easy our journey can be if we all work together.

Go into the woods and look at trees or throughout your day notice the different kinds of trees you pass by. What do you see? Right, you see trees. How many different kinds of trees do you see?

Do you notice the decay at all, the blight on the outside, the bugs on the inside? Do you know what kind of tree you are looking at? Do you feel the need to find out more about them – look up their names, characteristics, purposes? Or was simply noticing them enough to make you see their beauty and their worth? Isn't it easier to simply see the trees, without needing the specifics, and know that they are miracles?

Tomorrow take the time to look at friends, family, co-workers, and strangers the same way you looked at those trees. Accept their true beauty. Do not see their decay, or their blight, or the bugs that live inside of them. Simply accept they have a name, unique characteristics, and a purpose – just like you. Simply notice how beautiful they are – just like you.

Acceptance certainly is not easy to do every moment of every day. The point is we need to try, and when we find ourselves not loving and accepting someone we need to become aware and make a better choice. If we continue to see others as different and unworthy how will they not see us the same way? We need to choose love. Our peace, the world's peace, is at stake.

We don't have to like everyone and not everyone needs to like us. In fact, if someone doesn't like you, it's none of your business. But if you choose love, you choose to become someone who likes everyone regardless.

Any resentment we have towards someone we share with everyone. We talk about our pains, continuing to give them life, strengthening their energy, allowing those pains to grow. But if we let that pain go – share love with everyone instead, talk about love instead, give life to love instead – we strengthen love's energy, allowing love to grow, allowing us all to heal.

We are not different. We have all been through stuff. We've all been to the bottom and crawled in the dirt – just like you have. But my stuff isn't any better or worse than your stuff, and your stuff isn't any better or worse than my stuff. We are all alike.

This isn't a competition for who has the best suffering stories, or who has suffered the longest, or even who has pulled themselves out of the worst suffering. This is a journey and we are all on it together.

We are here, we were created, to love one another, help one another, show each other how to love, help each other find peace. A daunting task? Not at all. It's quite simple. It's simply a choice.

**Repeat this mantra all day today:
I love everyone and everything.**

I Forgive Myself and You

"Forgiveness is the fragrance that the violet sheds
on the heel that has crushed it."
– Mark Twain

"I can forgive but I can never forget." Forgiveness. I'm sure all of us can think of one thing, one big thing, we are still emotionally holding on to. We are still carrying the burden of a cheating spouse, a parent who abandoned us, a friend who betrayed us. So what is forgiveness? Close your eyes. Think of that one thing, that one big thing, right now. How does it feel? Where does the pain begin, behind the eyes where the sting is already coming? Where does the pain end, deep within your chest or stomach where the ache is sometimes unbearable? Take a deep breath and, as you do, feel the energy of that pain swirling through your body, mind, and spirit. Now hold your breath, feel the years of hurt build until you are carrying all of it in that one held breath. Now let that breath go, let all of it go – the pain, the hurt, the sadness. Feel your body emptying of all the negativity. Now smile, and breathe in again, this time breathing in joy and happiness, filling your body with love. And as you let *this* breath go, allow it to swirl around you, surrounding you will nothing but goodness and serenity.

That is forgiveness.

Forgiveness means we are allowing ourselves to forget. It means we are not allowing the pain to control anything we do or anything we are. It means choosing to take that first step away from the pain and never looking back. It means we have chosen love for both ourselves and the person we feel has wronged us. This is probably one of the hardest things for us to do, but it may be the most important.

In love, there is nothing to forgive. But first we have to tell our ego that. Our ego believes we need to understand everything. Understand in order to accept, understand in order to forgive, understand in order to love. No, we do not need to understand. I think that's actually the point. If all we need to do is love, what is there really to understand?

We have all made unwise choices. Choosing love means we admit those choices we made, often out of confusion, and once we confront them we begin to heal. As we begin to heal, we learn from those choices and begin to correct them. Some require apologies for correction; some require making restitution; but most require simply letting go. Recognizing what we aren't proud of and moving away from it is the giant step we need to take on our journey towards peace through love.

As with acceptance, forgiveness needs to start with us. We can't begin to forgive and heal others until we have first forgiven and healed ourselves for those same things. Once we learn to forgive ourselves, we will then begin to learn how to extend that forgiveness outward.

We let go of the hurt and are yet another step closer to peace.

I know how hard self-forgiveness can be; I struggled with it for years. Look deep inside yourself. What have you been holding on to, the big stuff, the stuff you've carried around with you, the stuff that became such a part of you that you forgot you even had the ability to let go of it? Let's start there. To get to the light, we need to have the strength to look into the darkness.

After my first husband and I separated, in December of 2001, I had a lot of forgiving to do. Mostly, I needed to forgive myself. I hated myself for staying with someone for eleven years who I knew I could never be myself with, someone I knew I could never be completely happy with, someone I don't remember ever even laughing with. I hated myself for wasting my high school and college years, so consumed with wanting girls to accept me and boys to like me, that I spent most of my time sitting by the phone or drowning in tears. I hated myself for spending more time pleasing others than figuring out what my own likes, wants, and desires were.

I hated myself for valuing others' opinions over my own. I hated that they didn't care half as much for me as I did for them. I hated myself for never becoming the world famous journalist I had dreamt of being. I hated myself for never pursuing any sort of writing career at all, my greatest passion since I was five years old. I hated that every poem I wrote, no matter how good it was, was filled with pain and heartache. I hated everything physical about myself. I hated my laziness after being energetic and active my entire childhood. I hated that the Red Sox losing felt like yet another betrayal and stab in my heart. I hated that I'd gotten sucked into the life of working in retail.

I hated myself for choices I'd made and secrets I forced myself to keep. I hated that I was alone, that the love I wanted simply didn't exist. I felt this way for years, giving in to joyful moments here and there. Friends and family did everything they could to keep me busy on the weekends. I hated myself for the pity they felt necessary to show me.

Those happy moments felt like a betrayal. How dare I let myself be happy? I didn't deserve them because of the choices I'd made. I had made such a mess of my life. I'd moved back in with my mother and spent most of my nights locked in my room reading.

Over the next year and three months, I read a lot of self-help books – some religious, some spiritual, some psychological. I wrote a little here and there. I also prayed a lot. I started realizing that, although I couldn't change or fix my situation or my ex-husband, I could change and fix myself.

In March of 2003, when my best friend told me the apartment across from hers was going to be available, I knew it was time to get out on my own and make a life for myself. I wasn't sure I was strong enough; in fact I cried my first night there, sitting in the middle of my empty living room. I was alone and terrified. I cried every night for a very long time. I spent the next three years horribly depressed. I didn't know how to get the life I wanted. How could someone so loved by friends, family, even co-workers be so miserable?

In late February or early March of 2006, I was sent on a business trip. I would be rooming with someone I barely knew. I was nervous and dreading the trip to the airport. When I saw Carol sitting at the gate waiting for our flight, I wasn't any better. What if she didn't like me? What if we had nothing to talk about? My fear quickly passed. By the time we boarded the plane I knew there was a reason we were brought together. Although I didn't know what that reason was, I was now excited to find out what the next few days would bring.

I cannot recall how we started talking about my "stuff," but put two women in a hotel room together in a strange city where they don't know anyone else, and a lot of stories can be told. I poured my heart out to her. Maybe it was perfect timing, maybe it was divine intervention. Or maybe I was simply shown immense love. Carol's counseling made me feel validated. To have a virtual stranger, someone you weren't paying a fee to, tell you how loved you were, how worthy you were, how important you were to the world? I cannot find the words to express the effect she had on me. I didn't know how life-changing those days would be.

Carol recommended the book *God on a Harley* by Joan Brady. I bought it when we returned from our trip. I read it, and then re-read it again that same night. I felt like I finally had someone who handed me blueprints. I knew that there was only one way to pick myself out of the hell I'd allowed myself to fall into. I needed to begin the excruciating process of forgiving myself.

I knew the first step was getting outside the confines of my locked apartment door. I'd spend my time over the next nine months doing things for myself. I would get in my car, and armed with a full tank and a map, I would just drive. I would find little shops that sold coffee or crystals or books. I would take my notebook and pen and find a park and write. I did a lot of soul-searching, thought about every awful thing I'd ever done or been through. I didn't do it with a sword – I did it with as much love as I could find. At first it wasn't a lot and it was hard, but I did it. It then became easier. I was already at rock bottom crawling on my hands and knees. Slowly I was rising out of the dirty sewers and was standing on my own two feet.

By December of that same year I felt reborn. I had forgiven myself and was finally at a place where I could now forgive my ex-husband. He'd done the best he could with what he'd been given in his own life. I focused on the things I loved about him; the things that made me love him at the beginning. He was caring, dedicated, a true friend. He was passionate about his beliefs, strong-willed. He had a very strong work ethic that I was always so proud of. Despite everything that happened between us – growing apart instead of together – these qualities are things that ego cannot change. These are the things I held on to, allowing me to finally forgive and finally heal.

My healing started because of the love Carol showed me. Her love, and the love I then chose to give myself, created a miracle – I found *me*.

"I had an abortion." You ended a life. You have tortured yourself ever since. It has consumed you. Maybe you turned away from friends when they had children so you wouldn't have to be reminded. Or you refused to have any children as penance for what you did. Or you became an overbearing mother who cannot let her children out of her sight. There are some who even believe our physical bodies reflect our emotions. Was that hysterectomy my torture for having an abortion? You ask why you deserve a happy, loving life when you took that away from someone else.

Why? Because you were made by love to be loved and give love, that's why. Every day is a new opportunity to remember that and move on. Perhaps you decide to work in a crisis center for teens so you can help someone else not have to go through what you have. Perhaps you choose to have an open dialog between you and your own teenage daughter so her choices are right for her. Perhaps you find a way to teach children or mentor them. Or perhaps you simply learn to let go. No amount of pain and suffering will change the choice you made. What's done is done. Choose to forgive yourself right now. Choose love.

"My addiction broke up my marriage." You chose your addiction over your marriage. Maybe you used your addiction to mask the pain and loneliness you felt by being married to the wrong person. Or the addiction was too powerful for your ego to ignore. Maybe you are choosing to continue the relationship with your addiction now that your marriage is over. You ask why you deserve a happy, loving life when you sabotaged someone else's.

Why? Because you were made by love to be loved and give love, that's why. Perhaps you check into a rehab program today. Perhaps you finally get the professional help that can carry you to the other end of your addiction. Perhaps you can tell those you hurt "I'm sorry for hurting you and I'm sorry for hurting us and I'm sorry for hurting myself." Or perhaps you simply learn to let go. No amount of pain and suffering will change the choice you made. What's done is done. Choose to forgive yourself right now. Choose love.

Forgiving ourselves is hard, so what about forgiving others? Once you forgive yourself for something, it is much easier to now start forgiving someone else. Forgiving others doesn't give them an out; it doesn't let them off the hook. Forgiving others doesn't make what they did right. But they are not the ones being punished by your lack of forgiveness – *you are*.

When we choose love, we choose to let go so our suffering can end. When we choose love, we also realize everyone has been hurt, everyone has suffered pain. No one's pain is better or worse than anyone else's. Pain is to you as it is to me. The more we forgive others, the more we heal ourselves.

Sometimes just saying the words out loud is a good start.

"I need to forgive the person who abused me." You were violated. You have lived with this memory every day. Sometimes you realize you haven't thought about it in weeks; sometimes it comes back to you in a split second unexpectedly. It has become the very foundation you built yourself around. Maybe you withdraw from ever having an intimate relationship. Or you were promiscuous, needing to create other memories to push this one down. Maybe you thought you rose above it; you are too strong to let this beat you – you've become controlling, self-absorbed, ego-driven. Maybe you take comfort in playing the victim – "As long as I'm still alive I've won." But have you? You have not won unless you have forgiven. And until you have forgiven, you cannot heal. And if you cannot heal, you cannot know love, and you can't find peace.

"I need to forgive my cheating ex." You feel betrayed, unattractive, unlovable. Maybe you said you would never trust again and withdrew from love. Or you became over-independent, needing to show the world how strong you are. Your ex has remarried and it just isn't fair. No, what isn't fair is the lack of forgiveness. Forgiving doesn't make the cheating right. Forgiving allows you to heal.

"I need to forgive my parents' divorce."

"I need to forgive my child for disrespecting me."

"I need to forgive the driver of the car that killed my friend."

Isn't it easier to let go than to hold on? Think about the rope you have been clinging to for so long. Aren't you tired of talking about it, reliving it? Aren't you ready to never give it life again? Release your grip. Allow yourself to let go, allow what you have been clutching to fall to the ground, and allow yourself to finally be free. Allow the miracle to happen.

Sometimes this step requires professional assistance; sometimes you can do it on your own. Try writing it out. Write down who you can't forgive and why. Be honest; write down all the bad stuff. Now write down how different your life is because of this person or incident. Write down the bad and now write down the good. Find *something* good. Maybe you realized things about yourself you needed to change and without this breakup you wouldn't have noticed. Maybe you wouldn't have the great marriage you have now if your ex-husband hadn't abused you. Maybe you wouldn't be the great parent you are now had your father not left when you were an infant. Notice all the good despite the bad, and maybe even in spite of the bad.

The greatest gift you can give yourself is forgiveness, both forgiving yourself and forgiving everyone else. You open up a space in your heart that you had filled with rage and resentment, and you can now fill that space with love.

Forgive yourself for holding on, and then start to heal by forgiving anyone who has wronged you. Forgive and we can start to change how we see ourselves and the world. Forgive and start making miracles happen. Forgive and we all find love. And once we find love, we will realize there might never have been a need for forgiveness in the first place. We are suddenly a little more at peace.

Repeat this mantra all day today:
I forgive myself and you.

I Choose My Mood and I Choose Peace

"Holding anger is a poison. It eats you from inside. We think that hating is a weapon that attacks the person who harmed us. But hatred is a curved blade.
And the harm we do, we do to ourselves."
– Mitch Albom, *The Five People You Meet in Heaven*

Most of us have heard – were even raised on the belief – that things happen "for a reason." Maybe they do, or maybe it's our reactions to them that give them reason. We can call anger different things – being frustrated, annoyed, irritated, upset, mad, outraged. We can react to anger by rolling our eyes, taking a big sigh, or huffing and puffing. We can yell and scream, throw things, even hit something. But all forms of anger have one thing in common – they steal away our chance at peace of mind.

When we get angry it seems justified. We feel the person we are taking our anger out on deserves our wrath for what they did to us or how what they did affects us. My question to you is this – do you feel better or worse when you get angry?

We know how bad anger is for our minds, but imagine how bad it is for our physical health as well. Our hearts race, we may even sweat, we can't sit still. I for one have experienced back aches and migraines, not to mention gastrointestinal issues, from carrying such burdens. Holding on to anger creates more anger. Changing anger to love creates more love. Not easy to do? Perhaps, but that's why they call it strength.

Are you the better person for getting angry? Are you angry because you're right and they're wrong? Are they are a bad person and deserve punishment? Yet who are you really punishing?

Every emotion and reaction we experience and give out to others is a choice. It is our own choice to either show anger or love. It is our own choice to either play the victim or set a different example. It is our own choice to either fight or walk away.

When you have a negative thought, choose to let it go. When you feel a negative emotion beginning to emerge, choose to walk away. It takes practice. But the more you do it – the more you see how much better you feel by letting these negative emotions go – the easier choosing love will become. And soon choosing love won't even need to be a choice; it will just be.

Someone cuts you off driving to work or takes the parking spot you were going after. If you get angry, what does that prove? If you yell at the other driver, what does that accomplish? Is either outcome peaceful to you or the other driver? Go back and redo the situation. Instead of getting angry, send love to the driver who cut you off. Be grateful there wasn't an accident. Remember that driver could be rushing to the hospital to see his dying father or watch his baby being born. Find another parking spot. Remember that driver could be older, have arthritis or other ailments, or could have just had surgery and they need to be closer. Choose love as your response and love will find you.

When we are angry at someone, it is often something that we actually see and don't like about ourselves. Think about that. Is it possible that all anger is doubt about ourselves? Go through your day and see how many times your peace is stolen away. Then ask yourself why.

Your partner didn't turn off the coffee pot. Have you never forgotten to do something that might have frustrated your partner? You get annoyed at a co-worker for making the same error over and over again. Have you never made errors that could have annoyed someone else? Was there nothing you were trying to learn that you just couldn't grasp quickly? You get upset at the cashier in the grocery store for texting instead of acknowledging you. Have you never ignored someone or not given someone your full attention in order to take a call or send a text or finish an email? If you stop and think about what you're doing and how it might be affecting someone else, maybe you'll remember we are all the same, and other people's small stuff will stop affecting you.

"Liars make me angry." Have you never lied, ever, about anything? We all have. But if someone is spreading a lie about you, remember that a lie isn't truth. No one can make you something you're not, just like you cannot make someone something they are not. Don't let anyone steal your peace, and when you choose love you will remember to not try to steal theirs. When someone lies, or you get caught in a lie, don't get defensive, just choose differently, choose love, be yourself, be true. Truth is just another word for love, because after all, love is the ultimate truth.

Is someone accusing you of something you didn't do? Do not get angry. Defend yourself with the truth. As long as you stay true to yourself, as long as you choose love all the time, you will keep your peace. You may be hurt; you may even lose a battle. But you will never even enter their war.

When you are angry it is usually not because of what you think you're angry about. Are you really angry at your co-worker for making the same errors over and over again, or are you angry that your training isn't working? Or maybe you are angry because the process isn't very smooth to begin with.

Are you really angry at your child because they didn't put their laundry away, or are you angry that your own laziness is rubbing off on him? Or are you angry that you haven't been able to teach him responsibility in general? Or maybe you are angry that he didn't put the laundry away at the exact time you wanted him to.

Choosing love doesn't mean not training the right way, not disciplining if you are a supervisor or a parent or even just a co-worker. Choosing love means responding with love – teaching correctly, giving guidance, leading by example. Teach your child how to clean their room and explain why procrastinating isn't a positive life skill. Offer to assist in the task and show them the way. Reward both of you with love and you will create a miracle.

"Disrespect makes me angry." Disrespect can cross many lines, including bigotry and ignorance, arrogance and pride. The most common form of disrespect comes from defensiveness. We hate thinking we are wrong or that someone else has a right to tell us what to do, and this often leads us to disrespect someone because we feel we need to stick up for ourselves. Again, how we respond is a choice. If someone tells us we are wrong, we need to stop and think. Is there a possibility we *are* wrong? If not, if it's as simple as "The sky is blue," "No, it's green," and we know we are right, we make the choice to either stay and fight and be angry, or let truth win out by choosing love and walking away.

And what if we *are* wrong? We get defensive because we want to be right, and all this does is create negative emotions for ourselves and others. Admitting we are wrong means we've chosen love for us all so we can all move away from the anger.

We don't like being told what to do, and we disrespect others because we don't want to be ordered around, or we don't think the person telling us has that right. In your job, if your boss tells you to do something, it would be disrespectful to not do it. Your boss is being paid to tell you what to do and you are being paid to listen and do it. If you are ethically or morally against what you are being told to do, then maybe it's time for a conversation between you and your boss, or you and your boss's boss. Or maybe it's time for a new job. But disrespect causes anger and causes both you and the person you're disrespecting to get farther away from love. What is easier? What is more peaceful?

Sometimes at work you get someone (who is not your boss) who thinks she knows better than you, so when she tells you to do something your pride takes over. Who are you to tell me what to do? That's not my job! Well, is what she is asking you to do something that needs to be done? If so, what is easier – doing it or helping to find someone else to get it done, or letting our pride get in the way by arguing?

What about in your personal life? Your parents or friends tell you to do something that you don't want to do. Ask yourself, why don't I want to do this? Am I being lazy? Do I have something better to do? Am I trying to take the easy way out? Do I want to lie to get out of it, and now I'll have guilt? Will it make me feel better? Will this help my friend? What does your ego answer, and then what answer do you get when you choose love?

"I get angry at my co-worker for making the same errors." Maybe your peer is incapable of learning what you are trying to teach him. Just because it makes sense to you, doesn't mean it makes sense to him. Find another way, anger isn't the answer.

"I get mad at my spouse for being so forgetful." Maybe you never forget anything. Getting mad at your spouse won't help her remember. Pointing out her shortcomings won't help her remember. Choose love – leave her a note, call her to remind her about her appointment. I do understand some people are not receptive to even loving, gentle reminders. So what is the answer? Certainly not anger or sarcasm or any other negative emotion. Choose love. Walk away, let it go. It is not your job to correct someone else's behavior. It is not your job to get them to an appointment on time or remember to buy milk and bread at the store. Your job is simply to love them.

Choose love instead. A more peaceful life will surely be yours. Your relationships will become easier, and maybe, just maybe, your wife will remember about your plans tonight. This is the miracle, the miracle that love created.

Hate is an awful emotion that grows out of contrary opinions and unnatural perceptions causing intense anger. Every day we hear of hate crimes by one group who disagrees with another, whether because of their sexual orientation, religious beliefs, the color of their skin, or a number of other untrue things we ourselves gave value to. These people are consumed by their hatred when they just see their brothers and sisters as different. They have yet to learn that we are all the same.

We even use the word "hate" as much as we use the word "love."

"I hate that song." That is your opinion. Someone loves it, maybe even someone sitting right across the office from you. They hear your comment and are now angry or sad. Your opinion is just that, your opinion, a lie you have made your own truth. But it is not true.

And think of how strong that word is: hate. Do you really *hate* that song? If you take one word out of your vocabulary before any other, maybe that's the word you start with. Try to go all day today without saying it, without saying it about *anything*. And then don't say it tomorrow. Correct yourself if you slip, but by all means, do your best to get rid of it.

Maybe it will be easier when you start really thinking about others before you speak, before you judge, before you put your ego in front of the love you could be extending instead. Someone isn't fond of something you love, and you've heard them say it and it's made you angry or sad. You know their opinion is not true because it is not true to you. You don't let them tell you what is true for you, so do *not* tell them what is true for them.

"I'm not fond of peanut butter." Someone loves it. Someone isn't fond of something you love.

"That woman at the store was irritating." Someone loves her. Someone isn't fond of someone you love.

Hate exists because our ego causes us to see each other as different, but that is just perception. The reality is we are all the same. We are all on the same journey, we all are afraid, and we all just want to be happy. When you hate, blame, seek revenge, or pass judgment you are giving life to your anger. You will never find peace this way.

Choose to give life to love instead. There is where your peace lies.

Imagine someone's reaction to you when you choose love over anger. There are people who may try to instigate anger, try to push your buttons. They are expecting a reaction, expecting anger, expecting defensiveness. And instead you respond with love. Instead you smile, say ok, say thank you or no thank you. They might have had a comeback ready, waiting for the perfect moment to cut you down further. You took that away. You allowed love to take over the situation and anger disappeared. You just created a miracle.

Tragedies can bring up many different emotions – grief, sometimes guilt – but the strongest of these is usually anger. School shootings, movie theatre massacres, fifteen-year-olds dying at football practice, eighteen-year-olds being diagnosed with thyroid cancer. These are things that happen every day. We can't explain them and we aren't meant to understand them. We ask so many questions but may never have any answers. The only answer we ever need is love.

On December 14, 2012, twenty first graders and six adults were killed in Newtown, Connecticut. This tragedy was felt nation-, even world-, wide. While the media reported the events and tried to make sense of a senseless act, an outpouring of love covered the quiet community of Sandy Hook. Soon, this love, rather than the hate, was the focus, became the headlines that we saw night after night.

Toys were donated to families at the holidays, pies were baked to nourish their hearts, snowflakes were made to adorn the walls of the new school the survivors would now call home. When the families of those lost came forward, this love was shining brightly. And through that love they found the strength to carry on, to move on, to pay that love forward creating foundations, museums, playgrounds – creating miracles.

Catastrophic anger that leads to insane acts such as the Sandy Hook Elementary School shooting needs to stop. And if we can't stop the acts, we need to stop the snowballing of anger that can follow. We stop it by choosing love over anger – every time. Stop being angry, even slightly, at your spouse, your children, family and friends who have hurt you. Forgive them all and choose love instead. Love will start fueling this nightmare instead of anger. And maybe, just maybe, tragedies like this will become less and less. Please. Stop allowing the anger to win. Choose love instead.

When someone hurts us or our loved ones, it is a cry for help. Help them by choosing to respond with love. If we have been here hurting one another, why can't we be here helping one another? We simply choose a different way. Does staying angry at someone change what they've done today? No. But perhaps treating them with love and compassion will change what they do tomorrow.

Choosing love means living life, finding the small miracles that still occur despite the pain. Grieve, get angry. Feel what you need to feel. But do not let these emotions consume you. Find a positive way to help, pray if that is in your belief system, donate money to fundraisers. Getting angry, depressed, violent, despondent – this negativity only gives further life to the horror and that's not what you want to do. What you want to do is give further life to the love and create more miracles.

We cannot ever think that we can change someone, heal the sick or the dying. We cannot think we can be judge and jury. We cannot think we can protect our loved ones from never getting sick or hurt. All we can do is choose to live our lives in love and peace in order to make the pain lessen and allow the healing to begin.

When we respond with anger we create more anger. So is it that hard to believe that if we respond with love we create more love? When you get angry, stop and think. You always make the choice either to listen to your ego and be angry, or to choose love and be peaceful. See the person who upset you as yourself, like you are looking in the mirror. What did they do? Have you never done that or something similar? Are you really upset with them over what they did or are you projecting your anger from somewhere, or someone, else? Is it possible that your anger is simply doubt about yourself? If what they did is so devastating, isn't choosing love the miracle? Accept yourself, accept them, forgive yourself, forgive them, choose love, and let go of your anger.

Every day *you* decide what kind of day you will have. What will your choice be today? Anger is causing our world so much pain. Start with yourself and change your anger to love. With practice, something that used to cause anger will become just another opportunity for us to choose love, create miracles, and find peace.

Repeat this mantra all day today:
I choose my mood, and I choose peace.

I React With Only Love

"The secret of life is enjoying the passage of time.
Any fool can do it. There ain't nothin' to it."
– James Taylor, *Secret O' Life*

There is negativity everywhere. From the office gossip and complainer to the rude customers and store workers to the self-involved cellphone users and drivers, our world has become all about us and never about anyone else. But what we say and do is often not a clear picture of who we are. We need to remember that, and remember the same goes for our brothers and sisters who we are on this journey with. In order to find peace, for ourselves and our world, we need to fill our lives with love instead of negativity, strength instead of weakness.

"Don't sweat the small stuff." Sounds simple enough, doesn't it? You'd be surprised at how many people don't even know what that means. They have absolutely no idea how negative they are all the time. They are emotional vampires, literally sucking the life out of, well, life! Constant negative energy is suffocating us, eating away at us, destroying our peace; even making us negative to negativity, creating chaos. It is this chaos that is leading us further and further away from love and peace, literally killing us. Choosing love means choosing to finally live.

If you're having a bad day, why choose to extend that negativity to someone else? Maybe they were having a perfectly fine day and because you treated them poorly they are now sad and upset. They then spread this negativity and it continues person after person after person and the world is filled with all that heartless energy.

Everything you give out you get back. If you yell at someone, you are disappointed in yourself. If you gossip about someone, you are guilty about your own self-inflicted shortcomings. If you complain all the time, you will never find peace.

Why not choose love instead? If you smile at the cashier who seems bored at her job, or give a good tip to the waitress who looks sad, maybe you have just turned their entire day around. They then pay that love forward person after person after person. And now, instead of all that angst, you have just created all that love. You have just created miracles. And love and miracles will come back to you.

How often do you have a negative thought? How often does this negative thought get spoken, get let out into the atmosphere, spreading like wildfire? This is difficult to acknowledge, difficult because as I stated above, most people can't even recognize when they are being negative. Or, if they do notice, they think being negative about the small stuff isn't their problem, but ours. They are just trying to be funny or get noticed or tell us we are just being too sensitive.

People who are always thinking negative thoughts often don't even realize it. They think others, and life, are constantly trying to hurt them. They cannot see that it is their negativity that is inflicting the pain onto themselves and everyone they interact with. We are so quick to tear down others, and until we learn to stop this, we ourselves will continue to be torn down.

Notice how often you are negative today. Notice how often your officemate is negative. Notice how often you overhear a negative statement or conversation. By the end of the day you may want to run screaming out the door!

But don't. Not yet anyway. You'll know when you have to if that time comes. But for now, find a better way. Choose love. How? Although tuning them out is the logical answer, it's not very easy to do unless you can wear headphones or earplugs. To start, ignore the negative statements. Don't fall into the negativity by asking questions or commenting. You'll be surprised how many of these conversations will end once one person chooses to let the urge to respond go.

Inevitably there will be someone who feeds the negativity and will keep the conversation alive and well. But one less person, namely you, who decides to walk away from it, shortens its life. Remember, this is about *you* choosing love. This is about *your* peace. You will see that someday soon, whether they know it or not, the negative people will speak less and less negativity. Or maybe you will simply notice it less. And that is when you will realize you made a difference. That is when you will have your miracle.

I used to think I needed to point out the negativity, correct people, show them the way to love. But being negative about the negativity isn't choosing love, it's choosing arrogance. It's me thinking I am a better person, thinking I can teach them by leading them. No, that's not choosing love. Choosing love means being an example of love, and being an example of love means staying quiet and letting the moment of negativity pass. There is negativity; there always will be everywhere you go. It is our attention and reaction to it that allows it to either fester and overpower our day or become an opportunity to create a miracle through love.

You get reprimanded at work for making an error. If you get defensive, how does that affect the rest of your day? Do you gossip and badmouth the boss? Do you compare yourself to the person doing the reprimanding? Now go back and redo the situation. Instead of getting defensive, think about the reprimand. Did you rush through your work, thus making an error? Did you put no effort into it, were you lazy or distracted? Are you angry at the person who reprimanded you? Are you angry at being reprimanded? Or are you really angry at yourself for making the error in the first place? In any case, choose love and move on.

Your co-worker is driving you crazy. He hasn't stopped gossiping, he continues to tell you what to do, and he is doing things wrong that he refuses to even acknowledge. Do you lose your cool and finally blow up at him? Do you disrupt your other co-workers by arguing in front of them? Go back and redo this situation. What is your response now? Do you simply let him talk as you move away, maybe going back to fix the wrong-doings later? Do you try to talk to him lovingly, hoping he will welcome the feedback? Do you talk to your boss and let her handle the issue? Is being right worth losing your calm? Is being right worth a hostile work environment? In any event, choose love. Choose what direction gives you both peace and doesn't fill either of you with anger. And then move on.

If you are the one making the errors, you need to admit them, listen to and accept others criticism. Choosing love doesn't mean neglecting your responsibilities or finding excuses why you could not give something one hundred percent of your time and effort. You need to welcome the advice and help your co-workers can give you. You need to know what is expected of you and learn to use all the resources given to you to do your job and do it well. Or maybe it's time to admit you cannot do the job and find a job you will enjoy and can excel at.

How many times a day do you hear the word "I?" How many times a day do you yourself say it? This is the ego talking. The ego wants us to feel special, unique, better than everyone else, deserving. Listening to the ego causes you to only hear and see the negativity in the world. Whenever the ego is in control you are not choosing love. And when you are not choosing love, you are losing peace.

"I want to give my opinion."

"I want to talk about myself."

When you focus on yourself, the entire world is against you. When you focus on yourself, you will lose your peace. When your focus moves to others, you will remember how alike we all are and you will care more about their well-being. When you are too busy being arrogant, you don't have time to listen to others because you are too busy talking about yourself. We feel we aren't somebody until people know who we are, until we are heard. We want to be liked by everyone, or at least most people. And if we don't care if we're liked by people, we still want them to think we matter. We have to tell vulgar jokes to make people laugh; we have to voice our opinion because ours is the only one of value or because it is the right one. When you choose love you stop needing to be the center of attention and you create a person instead who others simply want to notice. Stop trying to be somebody and just *be*.

When you choose ego you become controlling, a bully. You tell others what to do, what to think, how to feel, and when they don't listen, you respond with anger, bitterness, and resentment. Why do you think you are better than them? Or is it the insecurity that you feel you are *not* as good as them, and bullying them masks your own self-doubts? When you control others you do so because you do not want them to see your weaknesses;

you fear that they in turn will control you. Get over yourself. It's not about you.

Do you not follow rules you don't agree with? It's not about *me*, it's about *we*. And we are one. When the ego rules, it's about *me* – when and how will I be rewarded; who and what can I blame. When love rules it's about *we* – what is right for all of us; when and how will we heal; who and what can I strive to understand better.

"I don't talk on my cell phone at the movie theater so we can all enjoy the film."

"I don't speed or cut people off while I'm driving so we can all be safe."

"I don't argue with others so we can all keep our peace."

You can be a better person without being arrogant. In fact, not being arrogant is the only way *to* becoming a better person. And not being arrogant means becoming aware. The more you become aware – the more you see how important everyone is, the more you see the little miracles that come from choosing love – the less arrogant you will be. The more aware you are, the more you choose love. The more you choose love the more you find peace.

How often do you drag your negativity from one place to another, one person to another? You have an argument with your spouse, then have a bad day at work, then get cut off on the highway on your way to the store, then have your parking place get taken by someone else, and then you burn dinner. How often do you get in an argument with someone and then someone else and then again someone else? Had you not let that first bad incident affect you poorly, your entire day could have gone differently. Had you not taken it with you and then allowed all the other bad things to pile up on top of it, you could have found more opportunities to choose love.

When you choose love over ego, you learn to be respectful of everyone around you. You are no longer the source of distraction – talking in the movie theater or library, using your cell phone in a restaurant or other public place, driving fast or erratic with no consideration for the other drivers on the road. When you choose awareness over ego you notice everyone around you, even strangers walking into a building behind you who you begin holding doors open for. You respond to invitations that you used to ignore rather than simply telling your friend you are unable to attend their function. You stop bringing uninvited guests to weddings or holiday gatherings. You no longer tell your host what time you will be there, rather, you show up on time, or decline the invitation if the timing doesn't work for you.

You begin treating cashiers at the supermarket with kindness and a smile. You say "please" and "thank you." You stop expecting others to go out of their way for you, and you start going out of *your* way for others. You politely turn down something you really cannot do rather than ignoring the person who asked you for help. You are truthful; you do not lie to get out of a situation you are, or would be uncomfortable, in. You follow rules – you stop leaving your child unattended in the children's department of the local bookstore while you shop next store; you drive the speed limit and obey other traffic laws; you patiently wait your turn in line instead of fighting your way to the front.

Our relationships are in jeopardy. When we can take the focus off of ourselves and put it on, not only our loved-ones but also, every living thing we encounter, we will be setting the example of love. Once we do this, we lead the way for others to follow. And soon, the overbearing negativity will begin to dissolve and love will take its place as the norm.

Instead of blaming an inattentive spouse for your loneliness, ask them what they would like the two of you to do together, and then do it with a smile on your face and nothing – *nothing* – but love in your heart. The more you give instead of take, the more you will be given back. Choose your strength over your weakness.

Instead of being jealous that your grown children have their own independent lives, be proud of them for supporting their family values, owning their own home, having a steady and honest job and income. The more you show them love, the more love you will be shown back. Choose your strength over your weakness.

Instead of having self-pity and being a martyr and not asking for help out of pride, or instead of demanding someone drop everything to help you, simply ask someone to help you. And then thank them with words, or a card, or a kind gesture. The more you show yourself love and ask for help when needed, the less struggling you will have to do. Choose strength over weakness.

Do you have to comment on every Facebook, blog, or news posting? Do you need to be involved in every conversation and bring your opinion to every table? Do you get in a lot of arguments; feel like you always have to defend yourself? Do you need to know everything, know every secret, get envious if someone else knows something before you? If you are relying on other people for your happiness – Look at me! Give me attention! – you are not choosing love.

Stop playing the victim, looking for reasons and people to blame for your unhappiness. Your life is just that, *yours*. We cannot expect others to help us when we need help, but when we choose love we help them when they need it. We cannot expect our spouse to take care of the house and children alone, but when we choose love we set the example for what needs to be done. We cannot expect our parents or siblings to pay our bills or aid in healing our wounds, but when we choose love we assist whenever and however we can when our loved-ones are suffering. We cannot expect anyone to pick up the pieces to a mess that we and we alone created, but when we choose love we ask, "What can I do to help you?" And here's the biggest "cannot" there is: we cannot choose love and expect a reward. We will not be happy until we start giving service to others where the only reward is simply giving love.

We get back what we give out. If we give out love, we get love back. We cannot know nor have expectations as to how we will get that love returned to us, but the guarantee that it will be returned is truth. You help your neighbor shovel after a big snowstorm. Maybe they don't thank you or reward you the way you thought you deserved to be rewarded. But maybe the person in front of you at Starbuck's just bought your coffee. Or maybe you didn't hit one red light on your way to work so you weren't late like you thought you were going to be. You have received the love you gave out, just not in the way you thought you would.

When you choose love you do not ask people to give you something for nothing. They can offer it and you can accept, but you do not ask for it. You cannot ask people to go out of their way for you and you cannot be angry if they do not. But you should always ask someone if they need something from you and you should always go out of your way for someone if they ask.

We aren't perfect. The ego will win more often than we'd like. It is our job to notice when we aren't choosing love, be aware, and make the changes necessary. That is how we create miracles.

Go through your day acknowledging anything and everything that takes your attention away from love. Allow yourself to react. Do not reprimand, attack, or get angry at yourself. React, and if you do not like your reaction, or you know your reaction was not loving, forgive yourself, apologize, and let it go. Think about how you might react differently, lovingly, next time a similar situation arises. The more you do this, the more you won't have to think to react positively. The more you do this, the more your reactions will become more loving naturally.

Spread love to find peace. If someone threatens that, show them an example of love to follow. Even walking away instead of showing negativity is an example of love. And if we choose to walk away, our lesson always after is to never let it hurt us any longer. We have done our part, we have walked away in order to set our minds at ease.

Negative actions will have negative effects. Problems will continue to find us if we continue to look for problems. If we create chaos, chaos will be returned. If we create negativity, negativity will be returned. If we create love, love will be returned.

React differently today. Create only positive, loving conversations. Watch how you change the progression of your day. Do it again tomorrow. Watch how you positively change someone else's attitude towards you. And then do it again the next day. And the next. Watch how you change your life. Watch how choosing love leads the way to peace, not just for you, but for others whose lives you touch, often without even realizing it.

Repeat this mantra all day today:
I react with only love.

I Speak Only Truths

"If you tell the truth,
you don't have to remember anything."
– Mark Twain

The first and easiest way to notice lying is to listen to what comes out of our mouths. We lie in chat rooms and online dating services, pretending to be someone we aren't – someone older, younger, thinner, richer; someone funny, passionate, creative, successful. We lie on resumes to look smarter, more qualified. We even lie to get out of plans we made because we really didn't want to go in the first place. You will notice most of what we have become are lies.

How do you feel when you lie? Do you often have to lie again to cover up the original lie, or make the lie bigger so you don't look bad or the lie isn't found out? Go through today noting every time you tell a lie. This can be anything from telling yourself you are fat in the mirror while you're getting ready for work to telling your boss you aren't surfing the internet when you've been on Facebook all morning. Today, notice how often you lie. You will be shocked.

Don't worry about other people and whether or not they are telling the truth. You cannot know their truth.

Thinking they are lying is an assumption. Don't make assumptions; they aren't true.

Take tomorrow to try to not lie all day. It won't be easy. But if you choose love when looking at yourself in the mirror, you will not think you are fat, you will think you are perfect for where you are right now in your life. If you choose love you will not get into arguments with your co-workers about whose opinion matters most. Neither opinion is even true.

When the only answer you give is that of love, you are telling the truth. Notice when you lie and ask yourself, "Why did I lie?" Write it down, and write down what emotions you associate with why you told the lie. Perhaps you lied about being busy so your boss wouldn't make you help your co-worker. How did lying make you feel once you acknowledged that you lied? Maybe your truth is that you were being lazy, or you don't like your co-worker. Next time, remember to tell the truth. Tell your boss you aren't busy. Help your co-worker. The feelings of laziness and dislike will turn into feelings of satisfaction. Your weaknesses just became your strengths. Your lies just became truths. And as you tell more truths, the lies become less. And there miracles are made.

The biggest lies we tell are to ourselves. The biggest lies we believe are about ourselves. We believe we are sinful and imperfect. But we were born, made, created perfect. We were created out of love to love and be loved.

Love is the absolute truth. Truth is perfection. We are perfection. And that is not a lie.

One of the biggest lies we tell is expressed by us as guilt. Have you ever intentionally tried to make someone else feel guilty – your spouse, your friends, your co-workers? Do you compare guilt, see whose guilt is worse, have a competition on who can cause the most guilt, who can win whatever war you have chosen to wage? When you cause guilt in someone else you are lying. When we continue to lie, the guilt grows, expands. Worse, the guilt stays with us. And when a negative emotion stays with us, becomes part of us, we cannot find peace.

Wouldn't it have been easier to simply decline your friend's invitation rather than lying that you aren't feeling well? If they ask why you are declining, give them the truth, but then be ok with it. "I would like to stay home with my husband tonight." If they don't agree with your truth, don't get embarrassed or angry. It is your truth, own it. Whatever feelings they create from your truth – "She'd rather be with him over me." or "What does she even see in that guy?" – say nothing about you and everything about them.

You feel guilty because you are late to meet your friend. Why are you late arriving? Did something selfish get in your way of being on time? Find a way to let go of the guilt and next time you will be on time. Did something like a car accident get in your way of being on time? Did you help someone unselfishly? These were things out of your control, so there is no need for guilt. Let it go.

You feel guilty because a friend asked you for help and you said you couldn't. Are they asking out of their own laziness or selfishness? Then there is no need for your guilt. Are you saying "no" out of *your* own laziness or selfishness? Then forgive yourself, let go of the guilt, and maybe next time you will find another way and respond differently.

Truth *is*. There are no words needed, no actions taken. Sit quietly. Say nothing, think nothing. Look around. Have no opinion about what or who you see. That is truth. And truth will always win out, truth will always be exposed. Why? Because the truth is still there long after your lies have been told. You cannot avoid truth, just like you cannot avoid the ultimate truth – love. You cannot push the truth aside and hope it will go away.

"Romantic love stinks." This is your perception. Many people would tell you romantic love is beautiful. Of course, this is also their perception. The only truth here is that we all agree in love.

"Spiders are scary." This is your perception. Many people would tell you spiders are necessary, misunderstood creatures. Of course, this is also their perception. The only truth here is that we have all agreed to call that creature a spider.

"I am fat." This is your perception. Many people would tell you that your curves are sexy. Of course, this is also their perception. The only truth here is that we all have bodies and have chosen to give strength to opinions (lies) about what is and is not something we defined as "sexy."

"My ex-husband is a monster." This is your perception. Many people would tell you that your ex-husband is simply afraid. Someone even loves your ex-husband. Of course, this is also their perception. The only truth here is that we all see each other through different eyes.

What we see is only our perception of what we are looking at, and our perceptions are not truth. We see the world through our own judgments and scars, so how can what we see be real? We think romantic love stinks because we had our heart broken, not thinking about the endless number of lies we told ourselves about what romantic love is supposed to feel like. We think spiders are scary because they have so many legs and can be big and deadly, not thinking that we can overpower the spider or run away faster than it can catch us. We think we are fat because society has given us definitions of what is beautiful, not thinking that what matters about us is not what we perceive on the outside but what is actually on the inside. We think our ex-husband is a monster because he left us or abused us, not thinking that he left because he didn't think he deserved us; he abused us because he didn't want us to control him; that all the bad things he did had nothing to do with us and had only to do with his own fears about himself.

We have all had a break-up. Did you blame your partner or did you take on some of the responsibility? Did you see only what they did wrong but nothing that *you* could have done better? We have all had a job we didn't like. Did you blame the company or your boss for not being successful? If you were bored, did you ever try to find other work to do, co-workers to help, or were you too busy saying, "That's not my job?" We all have a family member we aren't talking to or issues that are not being discussed. Do you blame them for the disagreement or can you see where you overreacted? Were you actually wrong and they called you on it because it was easier than admitting you were angry about something that didn't even have anything to do with you?

Can you look back on any of these lies and find the truths? Can you learn something valuable about yourself? If you let go of the lies and guilt long enough to stop blaming someone else, and look at yourself and the situation with truth and love, I guarantee you will find the right relationship or the right job. You will be able to end the family troubles or walk away from them without feeling any guilt. If you continue to lie and blame someone or something else, you will never be happy.

Take today to be an observer. Notice your opinions and judgments and then throw them away. Try to see only universal truths, not societal opinions. Do not see a lazy co-worker, see a person who was made by love to love and be loved. Do not feel sorry for them, do not express pity, simply let them be. Better yet, offer them help or a smile, any act of love. Let the only truth you speak today, the only truth you act on today, be the only truth there is: love.

You cannot hate nor have a negative emotion when something is based on an opinion because all opinions are lies. Perceptions differ, opinions change. What is real, what is the truth, does not change. And that truth that never changes is love. Seeing the world through love is the only truth. Seeing people through love is the way to peace.

"My religion is the right one. Anyone who does not believe what I believe is wrong and they are going to hell." Religious or spiritual intolerance is not truth. Choosing love means not preaching to someone that their religion or their interpretation is wrong. Maybe the truth is that organized religions have different interpretations, different opinions that have changed since they began. Maybe the truth is that the one thing that hasn't changed, that one thing they *all* have in common, is love.

"My first husband worked all the time and didn't pay any attention to me or his sons." Maybe the truth is that he worked all the time to make more money because your spending habits were out of control. Maybe he didn't parent his sons because you were the one demanding their attention and going against everything he was trying to teach them. And now you're on your second divorce and blaming your second soon-to-be ex-husband for probably similar "faults". Where is *your* truth in all of this?

"My first wife was addicted to drugs and my second wife was addicted to shopping." Maybe the truth is that both created these habits to fill emotional needs that you were not. Maybe you were too busy going out with your friends. Maybe she was supposed to understand when you answered every call for help from your family and friends and children and she was always last on your priority list. And now you are divorced twice. Where is *your* truth in all of this?

Find the truths, no matter how painful. Find the truths in order to find peace.

"My boyfriend of six years cheated on me. After I got over the pain and anger, I realized what an awful girlfriend I'd been. We hadn't been intimate in over a year; we were more like best friends than lovers." You found your truth instead of blaming your ex-boyfriend.

"My first husband and I got married because it was the next logical step in our relationship. We had been together nine years and all of our friends were married and starting families. But we fought all the time, disagreed about everything. When we decided to divorce, we had grown up and apart and had different views on what marriage was going to be. I will never settle out of my fear of being alone, and I will never fight like that with anyone ever again." You found your truth instead blaming your ex-husband.

The lies we tell, we tell out of fear because we are afraid to notice the truths. You were too needy because of your fear of abandonment, but you blame the men who didn't want you instead. You were promiscuous because of your fear of never being loved, but you blame the men for using you instead. You lied because you were afraid to disappoint your friend, but you blame your friend for asking for help in the first place. You were lazy because you were afraid you wouldn't be able to handle the demands of success, but you blame your dead-end job instead. You live with guilt because you are afraid you cannot live up to the bar that you and you alone set.

Once you acknowledge that all your lies are told because you are afraid, think about what you are afraid of. Once you know what you're afraid of and see that it is not the truth, you will realize there is never anything to fear at all. Release yourself from the lies and start living your truths.

Do you tell yourself the lie that you are fat when you really afraid of been seen or noticed? Are you afraid of being beautiful so you do not eat enough? Are you afraid if you are overweight you won't be loveable? Are you afraid of being alone? When you choose love over lies you will no longer fear your body, you will see your beauty no matter your size, and you will realize that as long as you extend love to yourself and others you will never be alone.

Do you tell yourself the lie that you are not good enough? Are you afraid of failure or embarrassment? Are you afraid you will succeed and your friends and co-workers will see you differently? Are you afraid you will not be able to handle the responsibility of continuing to get better and better? When you choose love you will no longer fear success – you will have a strong work ethic, and you will be able to help your friends and co-workers succeed also.

Do you tell yourself the lie that the more material possessions you have the more value you yourself have as a person? Do you tell yourself the lie that the more clothes or shoes you have the more beautiful you are? Are you afraid if you don't have these things you will be unworthy or ugly? When you choose love you realize you are perfect regardless of where you live or what you are wearing.

Do you tell yourself the lie that because you are adopted no one will ever truly want you? Are you afraid of being unloved? Or worse, are you afraid of *being* loved? Do you tell yourself the lie that your level of happiness should exceed that of the parents who gave you away? When you choose love you realize that you and your birth parents are worthy of love and happiness, and that your birth parents did the best they could at the time with what they knew and what they had.

Do you tell yourself the lie that your children do not need discipline? Are you afraid they will stop loving you? When you choose love, you realize guiding your children with love will always lead to the truth. And sometimes that love needs to be tough.

Do you tell yourself the lie that if your child isn't an "A" student or the star of the baseball team he will not be happy? Are you afraid he will embarrass you or that your own legacy will be at stake if he does not succeed? When you choose love you realize guiding your children with love will always lead to happiness. And sometimes they can be happier being a chef rather than a doctor.

We need to stop being afraid. We need to let go of any guilt we harbor. We need to stop lying. When we lie we are focusing on what we *don't* have instead of what we *do* have. We focus on who our brothers and sisters *aren't* instead of who they *are*. We focus on who *we* aren't instead of who *we* are.

Choosing love means choosing truth over lies. Anything other than the absolute truth is unloving. Anything other than the absolute truth creates chaos for you and for others. Do not let the lies around you make you a lie too. Choose truth. Choosing truth allows us to be the true love we were meant to be and is the way we will all find peace.

Repeat this mantra all day today:
I speak only truths.

I Remember Nothing Before Today

"Without freedom from the past,
there is no freedom at all."
– Kishnamutri

We let our past dictate our lives. We hold on to past pains, failures and losses, thoughts and perceptions. We even hold on to past victories and joy, hoping to catch a glimmer of that happiness today. Choosing love means letting go of the past to find love and peace today.

Some of us hold on to the past because we think it makes us stronger. If we remember the troubles we survived, show others our battle scars, getting through today will be easier. We view letting go as a sign of denial or weakness. But if letting go is a sign of weakness, shouldn't it be easy? No, letting go requires much greater strength than holding on.

When we hold on to the past we are holding on to all the negative emotions like guilt, anger, and grief that go along with it. This will hurt us more than the actual event that caused those emotions in the first place. Letting go is what heals us and changes our life.

If we feel guilty, it is because we are holding on to past religious beliefs, moral judgments, or perceptions and opinions we created in the past that we have not let go of.

Choose to see the situation differently, through the eyes of love, and let go of the guilt today.

If we cannot forgive, it is because we are holding on to a past hurt that we believe someone caused us. Choose to see that person differently, through the eyes of love. Forgive them and move on.

If we are angry at someone or cannot accept someone as being our equal, it is because of labels or ideas we or others put on that person in the past. Choose to see that person with new eyes today, as if you are seeing them for the first time. No opinions, no labels. Choose to see that person through the eyes of love. See them today, not yesterday.

Why are you holding on, not allowing the holes to close? Do you feel your self-worth will decrease, that you will be seen as weak? Do you feel you will become less? Have you thought that maybe if you let go, you will actually become more? Choosing love means looking inside yourself, loving yourself, in order to fill the holes that you yourself have chosen to leave empty.

We need to deal with people from our past we cannot let go of in order to have a peaceful life. Make a list of people or past incidents you continue to allow to affect your life today. Write down the emotions you get when you think about them. That negativity has stayed with you, been eating away at your love and your chance at peace. Think of ways you have taken that negative energy and manifested it outward onto others. Know that you have the power, right now, to let those negative emotions go and stop the cycle of anger and hatred. You have the power to let go of the past and choose love instead.

My father walked out on my mother, my brothers, and me when I was just three days old. I lived my life with a fear of abandonment. I was boy-crazy and clingy, begging for love and companionship. I blamed my father for the poor choices I made, for every tear I cried, for every boy and man that left. One day I'd had enough. His past and mine had nothing to do with who I wanted to be in the future. I simply decided to start again. I decided to live just for today and tomorrow I would do the same. Yes, it really was that simple. I chose to let go.

"My friend didn't support me when I needed her the most so I walked away." But have you let go? Do you still talk about what happened, how hurt you were and still are? Get over it. Let go.

"I was raped when I was seventeen. I can never be with anyone again." Why not? You did nothing wrong. Why are you letting someone else steal you of intimacy and love? Letting go won't change any of his circumstances right now, but it will change yours. Letting go of the past allows you a new today and a happy tomorrow.

"I hate my birth mother for giving me up for adoption. I still think about it all the time." Why? Let go. You would not be who you are or where you are if she hadn't made that decision. Or perhaps you hate your life today and blame her for that. Why? Let go. Take responsibility for yourself. Letting go won't change the fact that you were adopted, it certainly won't change your birth mother's circumstances right now, but it will change yours.

Think about why people from your past were in your life, why certain things happened to you. What lessons were you supposed to learn? How has holding on to that past pain affected your life and relationships today? Do you continue to go through similar issues and relationships? If you hold on to pain you will continue to give out pain and continue getting pain in return. You need to let go and heal.

So many people blame their childhoods and their parents for their depression and failures. Our parents did the best they could with what they knew. They learned from their own parents. Forgive them. Times are changing. You are changing. Now that you know a bit more, are becoming a little more aware, choose to change the pattern. Take responsibility for yourself, your happiness, and the choices you have made or not made. Show yourself love and decide right now to forgive them for what you think they did to you, and forgive yourself for holding on to it.

Were you abused and now you are abusing, either physically or verbally? Was one of your parents a drunk and now you are struggling with your own addictions? Do you refuse to get into a loving partnership now because of someone who hurt you years ago? Were your parents strict so you are passive? Will you not try to conceive a child because of a past miscarriage or abortion? Will you not get into a new relationship because the love of your life left you or passed away?

Stop reliving the past. Start right now. Choose to change your mind and change your life today.

Not only do we not let go of people from our past who we feel have wronged us, we allow opinions we created and beliefs we've held onto to continue to be truths today. We were raised Catholic but haven't had a committed practice to it in years, yet we won't eat meat on Fridays during lent or we'll go to hell. We cannot believe anything that woman says because in fourth grade she told a lie about us. Even as an adult she must still be a liar.

We even hold on to past joys that keep us from being happy today and in the future. High school was one of the best times of our life because we tell ourselves we were prettier, more popular, captain of the cheerleading squad. We have the same friends and pursue the same kind of pleasures. Yet we're unhappy. We never changed, we never allowed the past to stay there, and so today never even had a chance.

If we judge ourselves or someone else in the past it inhibits our future and theirs. Choose differently. Choose love.

Ignoring your past isn't the same as choosing love and letting go of the past. You need to know what you're feeling and why in order to then let it go, otherwise it will continue to show up when you least expect it. The more you identify with your feelings and allow them to move away from you, the easier letting go of the past will become.

Whether it's losing someone we love, the house we grew up in, or our dream job, grieving can take its toll on us. Some days are too difficult to get through without tears, and the smallest reminder can set us on a path of pain. Our grief is often coupled with anger ("Why did this happen?"), depression ("How will I ever find anyone to love me again?"), fear ("What if I don't find another job right away?"), and many of the other negative emotions we are trying to learn to move away from.

So where does grief fit into this new thought process of letting go of the past and choosing love? The pain associated with grieving is very real and can last weeks, months, even years in some cases. How do I choose love when the hurt won't let go? It's not being apathetic, that's not what letting go and walking away from grief means. We have a right to be sad and mourn the loss of our loved ones and things dear to us. We need to learn to not let the other negative emotions surface and take over our lives during our period of grieving.

We need to allow ourselves to feel grief when we have lost a loved one or something precious to us. When we come to a point where we can accept what we're feeling and forgive ourselves for the guilt and the anger and all the other stuff that got in our way of peace, we find ourselves back at the sadness. Once we allow ourselves the sadness, we have chosen to heal. And choosing to heal means choosing love. And once we choose love, we can start to see the things that caused our grief a little differently.

Losing our house means having to move or rebuild. Maybe moving finds us living next door to a neighbor who changes our life. Or they end up being the man or woman of our dreams. Rebuilding gives us a stronger house. Perhaps we lost old photographs, our wedding and baby albums. Moving or rebuilding doesn't get any of that back. We grieve at the loss. But when we choose love, we realize that none of those items made the house our home. Love did that, and love doesn't die.

Getting fired or laid off is terrifying. But when we choose love we realize it can open the doors to less stress and more happiness if we look in the right places. After a year of being unemployed perhaps we learn that we used to spend frivolously, didn't save when we should have, and now we know just how much we can do on so little. We are no longer as materialistic, we have been forced to simplify and look within ourselves to find a strength we didn't know we had. Or we find ourselves changing careers and realize we are finally living our life's purpose.

But the worst grieving pain usually follows the death of a loved one. When we lose a parent or a spouse, a child or a friend, even a beloved pet, it's ok to feel like your heart may never be whole again. How do we move on? We need to allow ourselves the time to grieve. Everyone has a different opinion about where we go when we die. But one thing is safe to say: if we were made by love to love and be loved, and love doesn't die, then our loved ones will always be with us.

Remembering with love those who have passed is not the same as living in the past with them. Living in the past means continuing to grieve, refusing to bring that grief back to love. Choosing love means healing from that grief and allowing yourself to remember. We can do this by finding a way to keep our loved ones with us while we are completing the rest of our journey here. What did you admire about your loved one who passed? What was their passion? What comes to mind first when you think about them?

"My aunt was the most kind, loving person I ever knew." Honor them by acting as they did. Be kinder, more loving. Still talk to your aunt in your heart, ask her for guidance, and listen to the answer.

"My son loved baseball." Honor them by coaching a little league team. Donate to the new field they are trying to raise money for. Give a scholarship to an athlete at his high school.

"My mother loved gardening." Create a garden in her honor. Don't have a green thumb? Buy a special plant already potted and put it in a special place, perhaps with a wind chime or bird feeder near it. Put a stone bench in the most peaceful area of your yard. Go there whenever you need or want your mother. Feel her energy and her love surround you.

When you love someone, it is forever. When a loved one passes or we lose a pet, yes, we mourn. But our love isn't gone, it never dies. We take that love with us, we continue to love, we continue to get love back. You are love and no one can take your love away. Love is a reflection, something that you radiate out that no one can change. Love is eternal.

Grief can be overwhelming. We need to allow ourselves to feel the grief in order to get to the other side. Choosing love means choosing to heal. And once we start healing, we find peace.

If we hold on to pains, even joys, from our past we will get stuck there. We cannot heal and we cannot change. Choose to see your day and the people you meet through new eyes. And regardless of what happens today, let it go and see tomorrow fresh and new. And then do that again the next day. Get out of the past and allow yourself a peaceful today and a peaceful tomorrow. That is choosing love. That is the miracle.

Repeat this mantra all day today:
I remember nothing before today.

Thank You

"Piglet noticed that even though he had a Very Small Heart, it could hold a rather large amount of Gratitude."
– A.A. Milne, *Winnie-the-Pooh*

If the greatest truth is love, the greatest expression of love is gratitude. When we say "I'm sorry" we are admitting we made a poor choice, showing regret, admitting we hurt someone in some way. And that's fine, even necessary sometimes. But when we say "Thank you" we are making anything unloving – any poor choice or any awful hurt – into something loving, something that we learned from, something that helped us change for the better. When we show gratitude, we are choosing love and creating miracles.

Think of a time where someone apologized to you. Maybe your ex-husband finally apologized after years of making you feel like you were the only one to blame for destroying your marriage. You can certainly feel relief and a huge burden of guilt can be lifted off of you. But imagine him now showing gratitude instead.

"Thank you for showing me what is really important to me in a marriage."

"Thank you for allowing me a chance to be happy and in love."

"Thank you for being my best friend for the past ten years. Thank you for the memories we made."

"Thank you for helping me become a person I can finally be proud of, because without everything we went through, I wouldn't be who I am today."

You should feel more than relief, more than lightened of the heavy load of your divorce. You should feel proud. You should feel empowered. You should feel loved.

Now think of a time *you* had to apologize. Maybe you cut your friend out of your life for over a year because your depression was so overwhelming. When she took you back with open arms, no questions asked, you said, "I'm sorry." Yes, she showed forgiveness, friendship, maybe sadness at your pain and the time you spent apart, joy at your reunion. Tears were shed, mostly tears of pain and guilt. Now imagine instead of, "I'm sorry," you said, "Thank you."

"Thank you for still loving me."

"Thank you for allowing me the time I needed to figure out my life. It helped me think for myself without fear of judgment."

"Thank you for the harsh opinions you had before our separation, for in your absence I was able to feel their stings of truth. Instead of reacting I was able to learn from what you said slowly."

Had gratitude been shown instead of or even coexisting with an apology, tears would still have been shed. But instead of tears of pain and guilt, they would have been tears of joy and love. Your gratitude would have created a miracle.

Make a list of the important people in your life. Write thank you letters to them. Even send the letters! Express gratitude for what they have given you and brought to your life. Write letters to your parents, spouse, children, friends, other family members, bosses, co-workers, doctors, lawyers, pets. Write letters to them even if they have passed. Maybe you didn't show gratitude to them, or show it enough. Now is your chance.

Make a list of people who are no longer in your life because of a falling out or because you simply let go of each other and grew apart. Write letters to your past partners, friends, and co-workers. Maybe include people whose choices hurt you in horribly tragic ways.

Say "Thank you" to your birth mother for giving you up for adoption, because you wouldn't be who and where you are today if she had kept you. You wouldn't be married to the same person, have the same children, or the same friends and family. Say "Thank you" to your alcoholic father because without him you would not have chosen to never pick up a drink and will never end up like him.

Use only words of love in your letters. Do not say "I hate you" or "Why did you do this to me?" Say "Thank you." Think of lessons you learned from them, things you changed about yourself or your life because of them. See them through your new eyes of love instead of the old eyes of regret and hatred.

Maybe even write letters to things in your life that have hurt you.

"Thank you, Depression, for grinding me into the pit I was in because I realized it wasn't bottomless after all. Without you I would never have known how strong I really am. Without you I would never be able to fully support my best friend who is dealing with you now. Thank you for bringing true understanding to my life."

"Thank you, Unemployment, for getting me out of that dead-end job that I was miserable in. Without you, I would never have had time to write the book I'd always dreamed of writing. Without you, I would never have found my current job which gives me less stress and more time with my family and friends."

"Thank you, Bankruptcy, for showing me the true value of a dollar. Without you I would never have known how materialistic I was being, how my self-worth was caught up in the money I used to have. Thank you for teaching me about money management."

"Thank you, Divorce, for getting me out of a bad marriage. Without you, I would never have found the love of my life and be married to exactly the kind of person I'd always dreamed of."

Take today to be grateful. Wake up being thankful for a new day, the warmth of your shower, your coffee cup. Be thankful your car started, that you made it to work without incident. Be grateful for the job you have, the job you do, the people who appreciate you and benefit from you being there. Be thankful for your husband for doing the dishes or making dinner. Thank your food for nourishing you, your table for holding your plates and seating your family together. Even thank your television for providing you with pleasure.

Learning to be grateful for every single thing this life and this world gives you will help you see every moment as important, as a chance to choose love and move you closer to peace.

Repeat this mantra all day today:
Thank You.

All That Matters Is Right Now

"So close no matter how far. Couldn't be much more from the heart. Forever trusting who we are. And nothing else matters."
– Metallica

When you choose love, letting go of the past and extending gratitude for your life and the people in it, you learn to live in the now. Living in the now means never looking back. And to journey towards peace, to really start living, you also need to stop looking ahead. But what you are doing right now does influence your future, so make what you are doing now a step in the right direction. You want to be moving forward, but moving forward now. Not tomorrow, not for tomorrow, but for now. Because *now* is all that ever matters.

When we think about our future, we worry. We worry about what others might think. We worry that we will look stupid, that we will be powerless. In high school we worry, "What if I don't get into college?" In college we worry, "What if I don't find a job in the field I majored in?" In our jobs we worry, "What if I don't make enough money to support my family?" "What if I don't get that promotion?" As young adults and older we worry all the time, sometimes obsessively. "What if I never get married?" "What if I never have children?" "What if my children aren't smart or healthy?" "What if my car breaks down?" "What if I fail?" The list goes on and on.

We have been told we need to work harder and harder to gain success. But what about joy? What price are you willing to pay for your happiness? We juggle work, our spouse, our children, our social lives. We multitask at work and at home. And it's killing us, stealing every opportunity we all have at peace.

Worry creates problems that don't even exist. We are making up things in our head, making mountains out of molehills. Sure, bad things have happened to us in the past, but we aren't living in the past anymore, remember? The past isn't real, the future isn't real. The only reality is right now, and now has no place for worry.

People will tell you they are looking ahead because they are "realists." What is real about imagination? Because worrying about the future is simply that, your imagination. You are making it up, it isn't the truth; it isn't real. If you think about it, time means nothing. Time is something we made up, so the emotions that go into our anxiety about time are pointless. Let your life happen naturally, with the natural laws of the universe, without you trying to make them happen.

Any time we try to go against the natural law of things it causes chaos. Any time we try to go against the natural law of things we are being arrogant. Watch animals or birds or even insects. They just *are*. They respect the laws of nature. They don't panic, they react.

Animals don't stress or overanalyze, they survive. They don't try to control anyone or anything. They don't try to change one another or turn one another into something they are not. They live harmoniously. They simply exist. They exist simply. And they still get things done.

What is natural law? Perfection? Being in tune with the universe? Maybe a better – no, the best – description is "love". When you have love, everything flows like a smooth river. A cloudless summer day. A clear, star-filled evening. Nothing is wrong. Everything is peaceful. Doesn't this love far outweigh the "evil?" The bad stuff – the anger, the negativity – is so minute, yet you feel it enter your peace immediately. Something doesn't feel right. Something is off. Love isn't flowing smoothly.

It is crucial during times where you feel bumps in the road to be aware. Understand what is causing your love to run off-course and stop it. Simply stop it. You know in your gut that person isn't right for you. Walk away. You know that job will never feel comfortable. Find a new one. You know right from wrong. Forget where you work and who you work with. What feels right? Helping someone or ignoring them? Doing the best you can or being lazy? Being happy or being sad? Choose to do the right thing. Choose love. You know how to turn the bad into the good. Walk away. Choose love and peace will follow.

Light is defined (Merriam-Webster) as "something that makes vision possible." Darkness is defined as "the absence of light." Light is the natural law; darkness is something we made up when we forgot to see the light.

Love is defined as "an assurance of affection." Hate is defined as "intense hostility and aversion usually deriving from fear, anger." Love is the natural law; hate is something we made when we forgot to see love.

Peace is defined as "a state of tranquility or quiet." War is defined as "a state of hostility, conflict, or antagonism." Peace is the natural state; war is something we made up when we forgot to see peace.

When you choose the laws of nature, when you choose love, you have fewer accidents, less falls, less pain. You have no doubts. You attract better energy, better people, better physical health. When you choose love, you attract love.

What used to be called nervous energy when I was a child manifested into anxiety as an adult. I have suffered from insomnia, clenched my teeth, picked at my nails. My head was constantly spinning. When it wasn't buzzing with worry and doubt it was repeating songs over and over and over until I thought I was going crazy. I even have a constant ringing in my ears that gets worse as I get older.

I am very sensitive to noise, something that also gets worse as the years go by. I realized one day that I need to step into the quiet, not just once in a while when I feel the world overwhelming me, but every day, no matter what kind of day I am having. The more I made this a daily practice, the more these nervous habits started becoming less and less. And when I find myself picking at my nails or clenching my teeth now, I am aware and I stop. I let go. When I can't get a song out of my head I acknowledge it and let it go. I don't even put the radio on in the car anymore. I have become an observer.

When you live in the now, you respond to moments. You are present. Accept life, realize you cannot change some circumstances, live your life now instead of always trying to fight the past or the future. Notice what you can handle and be okay with it. If the evening news distresses you, stop watching! You can stay informed and in touch in other ways, ways that won't cause you to lose your peace.

Our lives are filled with unnecessary distractions that take our attention away from living in the now. There are so many choices and decisions we have to make and sometimes the smallest and easiest ones seem extraordinary when we are surrounded by so much noise and chaos.

Why aren't we spending time with our loved ones? Are they where your love should be? Are you choosing work over them? Friends? Perhaps it's time to cut back on your work or find a new job or go out with your friends less. Perhaps it's time to choose spending time with your loved ones over being in the PTA, or being on the board of your son's soccer league, or baking for yet another fundraiser.

The biggest distraction we have is ourselves. We talk all the time. We comment on everything, we have a voice and we want to be heard! When you choose love you decide that it is more peaceful to stay silent. We don't need to tell everyone everything that happens to us. We don't need to comment on every song that comes on the radio or after every phone call we make.

When we talk less, we are less critical and less negative. When we talk less, we listen more. When we listen, we live in the now. When we live in the now, we are more accepting of ourselves and others. When we live in the now, we are happier. When we are happier, we find love. When we find love, we want to spread more love to others. When we spread more love to others, we find peace.

We turn on the radio as soon as we get in the car. We turn on the television as soon as we get home. We're constantly texting, trolling the internet, playing electronic games. Even reading at times is a distraction, taking us away from what is real.

Stop checking email, turn off your phone, walk over to your co-worker instead of calling or emailing. Don't turn the radio on in your car on the way to work. Take the headphones out of your ears. Park your car a little further away and be aware of everything you walk by.

Pick up your feet when you walk. Walk with your head held high and your shoulders strong. Make eye contact. Smile.

I'm not saying never listen to music; sometimes music is the only thing that drowns the ego out long enough to relax us. I'm not saying never watch television, or text, or play on the computer. I'm saying simply to give them all a rest once in a while if they have been distracting you from living a life of love and peace. One hour a week, even one hour a day, turn off all your electronic devices. Put away your computers and phones, turn off the television and radio, put away your games and books. Spend time, real time, with your family and friends, in your garden, hiking in the woods, painting or running or dancing. Spend more time doing the things that make you happy. The more you feel you need a distraction, the more you will benefit from the silence and realize how much more peaceful your life is.

When someone or something tries to steal your peace, notice it, become aware. What feels better, more natural – to be angry with someone or to love someone? When you are burdened, close your eyes and go to the quiet. Simply be. That silence is now, that silence is love, and it will surround you. Smile, lighten your heart, breathe. Live in the now, joyful and carefree. All that is right and real is in the silence. When you retreat to the quiet, the truth stays. What is a lie goes away.

You must take yourself away, even if just for brief moments, from the noise that surrounds you. You need to remember who you really are, who your brothers and sisters really are, what this world really is. If you do this consistently, make living in the now a habit, then you will remember love, and you will find your peace even in the midst of the loudest chaos.

Making quiet part of every day will help keep you centered in the now and will be life-changing. Don't make excuses why you can't because those excuses are lies. If finding peace is truly what you want to do, you need to make it a priority. Take ten minutes in the morning. Start by sitting with your coffee and listening to the birds or just watching the world for a while. Water your flowers. Take a walk. Concentrate on your breathing. The quiet will help you focus, be less forgetful, less irritable. The quiet allows you to become more aware. It allows you to hear your inner voice.

If you can't step into the quiet easily, soft music may help. You can get absorbed into your awareness and it will take you to that same quiet place. When you realize how great you feel after just a few minutes, you will do this practice again in the evening. Ten minutes will extend to thirty. Then you'll find yourself looking for time for the quiet – during your lunch break, at the red lights you drive up to, in your car for an extra minute before you head into the house or work. You will be able to call the quiet when you need it. And in that quiet you will find peace.

You will soon find yourself living in the silence. You will comment less, if at all, when others start to gossip or chatter endlessly. You will have no opinions that are intended to hurt or shame another person. You will smile, love, exemplify joy. You will listen without judgment, noticing how situations become more peaceful, more loving. You will realize how much you don't need to listen to the ego. The ego, that once defined you, will weaken. You will realize that the silence, the truth, the love, is much more powerful. As you become more and more aware, you will know beyond a doubt if you are on the right path. Every answer to every question can be heard if we just take the time to listen.

Living in the now does not mean not doing anything. If you do nothing, nothing will happen. It means letting go of doubts from your past and worry about your future. Do something, anything, to keep you in the now, because doing something is the only way anything will happen. And maybe taking a few minutes a day loving yourself enough to sit and listen is exactly what you need to keep from hiding away from yourself and the world forever.

When you listen, you will think clearly. You will find a new way to do your job or know beyond the shadow of a doubt it is time to find a new one. You will no longer be impulsive.

As choosing love becomes more and more your natural habit, people may start asking you, "What's wrong? You've been so quiet." And you can answer, "Nothing is wrong. In the quiet, everything is right."

You are that voice of pure tranquil awareness that is your true self. Listen to the voice that tells you there is a better way. That voice is the one you need to listen to whether you call it Awareness, the Holy Spirit, God.

Take a morning, afternoon, or better yet a day for yourself. This isn't selfish or arrogant. We need to be in touch with ourselves, know who we really are. We need to know how to listen to our inner voice, to learn to love ourselves and others without conflicts or distractions.

Experience today in the now. Don't rush, don't think about the next place you have to be or someplace you "should" be instead of being here, now. Go to a peaceful place. Notice everything about your peaceful place. Wherever you are, just observe. See everything, really notice everything, as if experiencing it all for the very first time. Listen. Hear everything as if you are hearing it all for the very first time. Feel everything as if you are feeling it all for the very first time. Take in the aromas as if you are smelling them all for the very first time.

If you come in contact with people during your day, remember you are seeing them now for the very first time. If you run into someone you know, remember you are seeing them through new eyes. You have no past with them. This is an interaction you are having right now. Treat them as you treat your peaceful place and all you saw, heard, felt, tasted, smelled. Treat them with simplicity. Treat them with love.

At the end of your time alone, think about how you feel. Did you learn anything about yourself, how you interact with other people, the world? Think about how you call on this tranquility wherever you are, whenever you need it. You can make this peace a part of your everyday life.

Isn't it easier to be aware, without rushing through life concerned with the past or the future, concerned about what others think? Isn't it easier to simply see the world and how you react to it, feel about it? Isn't it easier to go through life living right now? Isn't it easier to take away your distractions?

Learn to live quietly in the now. You will find peace. What you will hear in the peace is your awareness that knows your ego and body are not who you are. That is truth, that is you, that is your essence. Call it what you will – your inner voice, the Holy Spirit, intuition, guidance. We all have it, we have just forgotten how to use it, how to call on it when we are in need. Using this guidance means listening to the natural laws of the universe. Our path will become so much easier when we realize we hold all the answers right here inside of us, right now.

Repeat this mantra all day today:
All that matters is right now.

What I See Is Not Who I Am

"You do not have a soul. You are a soul.
You *have* a body."
– C.S. Lewis

The physical body is not who we are. It is simply a shell that allows us to perform the tasks we need to in order to learn the lessons we are supposed to. When you choose love, the more aware you are, the less ill you will feel. You will begin to live who you are, not what your body is feeling.

Choosing love doesn't mean you will never have physical ailments, but you will not have them as often. Choosing love doesn't mean ignoring symptoms and not going to the doctor for treatment. Choosing love means not dwelling on your ailments. Choosing love means doing what feels right to get better. Stay calm and listen to what your body is telling you. Take care of it and respond to your body with love.

When you feel pain or discomfort, look beyond your ailments, change your view. Feel it, experience it, but do not give into it. Ask yourself why you got sick or hurt your back. Find an inner solution. Our mental struggles can definitely manifest into physical stress on our bodies, causing our disease. *Dis-ease*. Our ease, our peace, is being compromised. The next time something causes *dis*-ease in your life, ask yourself why you feel bad.

If your back hurts, ask yourself, "Am I carrying a heavy burden?" "Is there extra stress in my life at this moment?"

If you get a bad cold, ask yourself, "Am I holding on to something that I need to let go of?"

If you get the flu or another bedridden virus, ask yourself, "Have I been running myself ragged? Is it time to slow down and rest for a while?"

If you break a bone or find yourself immobile, ask yourself, "Do I need a break from something physical I have been doing? Do I need to focus on lending a hand or a shoulder to lean on? Do I need a stronger leg to stand on with a certain issue in my life?"

We are more than our physical body. But we are more than our ego-driven mind also. Who we are is that awareness behind the ego – the one who knows it's time to change, to stop being overwhelmed, to pick ourselves up off the ground when we've hit rock bottom.

I cannot go any further without talking a bit about depression. Depression is a disease. What is great about that is that we can overcome it. I would bet most of you who decided to pick up this book did so because you have been trampled by depression at one time in your life and never want to go back there again. You have decided to choose love instead.

I've been there. It was terrifying, sad, lonely, and mind-numbing. I am grateful for it every day because without it I would not be where I am today. The greatest lesson I learned was that, when you're down, sometimes you need to feel the pain in order to find the strength to pick yourself back up.

One thing didn't cause my depression. My divorce was the tipping point, but what caused it was me. I hated who I'd become. Every choice I'd ever made seemed to be the wrong one. I would be so good at something and then just stop doing it – softball, playing the flute, writing. My priorities were jokes, lies. In fact, I felt that *I* was a lie. When I looked in the mirror I had no idea who was looking back at me. Here I was at thirty-three years old and the last time I could honestly say I felt like me – the last time I stood up for myself, liked myself, felt real – was when I was fourteen.

I was on medication for a little while. I felt worse and gained twenty pounds so I got off of it and went years again without it. I tried psychotherapy but never stayed with it. When I decided I'd finally had enough of the misery, I tried an energy healing. Around this same time I'd simply started meeting people, virtual strangers, who seemed to understand and want to help. Not family, not friends, just people. I started reading and journaling. I also started writing down my dreams and trying to interpret them. I started feeling my feelings instead of trying to ignore them or feeling guilty about them. I became friends with my depression and chose to find its purpose. I started to do things for myself and by myself, and when I was ready I went on medication again. I knew I couldn't talk myself out of the final stage of depression I felt I was in. On the new medication, I was able to see more clearly than I ever had.

I no longer take medication although I still have days I want to crawl inside a dark cave and not come out until spring. But I no longer *suffer* from depression. Because depression is not who I am. I am better than that and I found the way that worked for me to get to the other side of it. If you suffer from depression, choose love. Choose today to get the professional help you need to realize you are so much more than the *dis*-ease inside your body.

During my depression I began to consciously start choosing love. It wasn't easy, but as I continued to move forward through it, it became easier. Even after depression was no longer defining who I was, I realized choosing love was still having a detoxifying effect on my body. I was stirring up old habits, emotions, and dirty water. I realized changes needed to be made. I realized I was becoming irritable and impatient with others who were not walking the same path of self-discovery.

You may feel these things too when you start choosing love, whether you've suffered from depression or not. Any old baggage can get reopened, even after you thought you'd long ago discarded it. You may be more tired and may even become physically ill for a short time. For any of you who have ever done a physical body cleanse, you know this is normal, and it is no different for an emotional cleanse. Your ego is fighting with your true self, but love will win. Love always wins.

This emotional detox stage doesn't have a time frame, so bear with it. It can happen dramatically and quickly, or it can happen slowly over many years, but often it is a combination of the two. You may have started detoxing years ago without even realizing it. Allow yourself to feel these emotions; don't get angry or upset, just get through it.

When you start to simplify your mind, you will notice how much other clutter you have in your life. You will feel detached from physical things that no longer matter like they used to.

Your desk at work is messy and disorganized. Go through each item and ask what its value is. Can you file it away, move it on to someone else who may have a need for it, or can you throw it away altogether? Get a new pencil cup, weed out your filing cabinet, clean up the dust bunnies behind your computer monitor.

Your office at home has become a catch-all. Get new shelving to organize the pile of books you've been meaning to read. Books you said you'd never part with you find yourself donating to the library book sale. You find the perfect wicker basket to store the magazines you haven't gone through yet. You finally throw out last decade's cancelled checks and pay stubs.

Walk through all the rooms in your house. Open drawers and closets. Really see each item you come across. Does it give your life value, worth? Can you let it go, give it to someone who could benefit from it? Has it served its purpose? You've accumulated countless knick-knacks over the years. You get boxes and start taking them down, wrapping them up to store; maybe you'll have a tag sale. Or maybe you take them to the dump and get rid of them all together.

Your closet is filled with clothes in three different sizes. You bag up everything you know you'll never wear again to bring to Goodwill. You get plastic totes to store the size you *know* you'll get back into one day and bring them to the attic. You will donate those too if you aren't into them in a year. In the attic you notice all the Christmas lights you've kept even though you know they don't work. You bag them up and bring them to your garage. What a mess! You order a dumpster to be delivered for the weekend. The list goes on.

After you've uncluttered your "stuff," you ask yourself if your life is cluttered. Have you over-extended yourself, your spouse, and your children? Make a list of what you do, what you have committed to – every club, committee, sons and daughter's sports and activities, book club, etc. Ask yourself the same questions – are they of value? Do I need them for my own self-worth? Ask your spouse and children to do the same. It is ok to let go of something that no longer has meaning in your life. What are you willing to give up in order to gain peace of mind?

You will also find yourself reevaluating people in your life. It is ok to let go of someone whose time has come and gone. Egos are drawn to one another, whether in love or in pain. Once you begin to choose love, you will begin losing interest in unloving egos and will become attracted to loving egos.

Maybe it's not so easy to listen to your friend of twenty years anymore. You realize how negative she is, how the world is constantly against her. The phone calls with her start to get a bit shorter.

You think about the guy you've been dating and what a struggle that relationship can be sometimes. You realize you can no longer stay with someone that just doesn't satisfy your emotional needs.

You've always had so many friends and something to do every night on the weekends and now none of that is appealing. Maybe you would rather be alone for a little while doing things *you* like to do, or finding new things you didn't yet know about yourself.

After college, my best friend and I worked together, played together, partied together. We were pretty much inseparable. I thought she would be my best friend forever. I couldn't imagine my life without her in it. We were maids-of-honor at each other's wedding. I became Godmother to her daughter.

Two years after I got married (the first time) I realized what a mess I'd made of my life. I felt very alone. I realized I had never been his priority, always an afterthought. I seemed to not fit anywhere in his life, like I was just along for the ride whenever he wanted me around. I realized I felt that exact same way when I was with my best friend.

We would make a date to spend time together, but it never worked out. She would always have to cancel or cut our time short because of another commitment she'd made to someone else. When my first husband and I separated, she wasn't there emotionally for me at all. I wasn't fun to be around by any means. I cried all the time and was just plain miserable. But a best friend is supposed to be there for you no matter what, right? Other people found time for me, wanted to help me get over my grief. But a year later, on the day when I left my mother's house to move out on my own, it was the beginning of the end of my friendship with her.

During the last year of my friendship with her, another woman came into my life. I was depressed, my marriage was in trouble, I felt abandoned by my best friend, and I had just started a new job. My new best friend was about seven years younger than me, newly married, and very strong and independent. She went after what she wanted and usually got it – personally and professionally. I admired her for being so young yet so grounded. She was the exact role-model I needed to pick myself back up. She and her husband brought me into their family and their lives, and I was truly blessed to find people who cared so much for me when I was so low.

For the next three years she helped me find *me*. She helped me grow in strength and individuality. I remembered the person I used to be and found the adult

I'd been longing to be and I will never forget what she brought to my life.

As important as she was on my journey, after a few years, our friendship, at least for me, had run its course. I felt that once I became the strong woman I needed to be, she treated me differently. Or maybe she treated me the same and I perceived it differently? I think she enjoyed counseling and encouraging me, and once I no longer needed that, she didn't enjoy our friendship. I know I didn't. In any event, she wasn't meant to continue to be a part of my life.

Sometimes people aren't meant to stay in our lives and we are not meant to stay in theirs. They were in our life to teach us a lesson or we were in theirs to teach them. We all served our purpose, played our part, and the time came to let go. And that's okay.

There may be some people who view you as selfish during your detox. You are taking so much time for yourself, you are declining invitations instead of saying "yes" to every one of them, and you are finding things other than them to fill your time. Be loving and tell them the truth. Tell them why you're doing this and where you want to be. Some of them will support your decisions and enjoy the ride with you. Other friendships may have run their course.

You may even begin to realize you're losing weight. All of a sudden the need for that ice cream or brownie is no longer there. You begin taking in food that is good for you because you are feeling so good mentally. You have more energy and find yourself parking farther away to enjoy the longer walk into the store. You dust off your running shoes and your bicycle. Instead of sitting in front of the television every night, you realize you don't need that escape from reality and you go for a walk outside. There are other things you are now gravitating towards.

Once the emotional detox starts to wear off, you realize how light you feel, how simple life has become. The more you simplify your thoughts and your life, the more you have – more love to give yourself and others, more time to spend on love instead of cleaning or cooking elaborate meals or doing yard work to keep up with the Joneses.

What you once thought would be boring is now what you look forward to. You realize life isn't about how many friends you have or how many material possessions you've acquired. It's not about running around, always being busy, always going and doing. You realize life is about peace. And you realize that by getting rid of all the excess, you suddenly have more, much more, than you ever imagined.

When we begin to choose love over ego, our bodies react, sometimes violently. This is our physical body's way of demanding attention. It doesn't want us to forget about it! Which we won't, how can we? It's with us everywhere we go. But when we choose love we realize that physical body is simply a vessel that our awareness is using. When we choose awareness over body, we are choosing love. We realize what we see is not who we are.

Repeat this mantra all day today:
What I see is not who I am.

I Believe

"We all have our own life to pursue, our own kind of dream to be weaving, and we all have the power to make wishes come true, as long as we keep believing."
– Louisa May Alcott

Most of my life I struggled with my spiritual beliefs. Although baptized Catholic, (even confirmed as an adult), my family did not practice. My mother was raised under strict Catholic beliefs, but when she went to her priest for solace after my father left, the priest asked her what *she* did wrong to make her husband leave. She was excommunicated for being a divorcee and she never returned to the Catholic Church.

Growing up I went to friends' Bat and Bar Mitzvahs, to Catholic masses, weddings, and funerals. None of those events ever left an impression on me beyond "I don't fit in here."

One of the first questions I remember having about spirituality or religion or whatever you decide to call it for yourself was, "What if all of this life and our world is just some big guy's dream?" Pretty profound for a five-year-old.

My mother did take us to a Christian fellowship church when we lived a few years in Arizona when I was five, six, and seven years old. I remember very little, but my most vivid memory is that we got bread – real bread! – at communion, and even the children were allowed to sip from the cup of wine. I remember people speaking in tongues, and I remember my mother being very happy. Peaceful.

My mother never spoke about religion at home except to say that she did believe in God, as did my grandmother, who I was very close to. At the time I had no idea what that even meant: God. But over the course of 30+ years, not belonging anywhere, feeling unworthy of belonging anywhere because my beliefs just didn't fit in anywhere, I became at peace with all of it.

I don't know when it happened, but it's safe to say it did – I slowly realized I didn't need a label to be spiritual. I didn't need some doctrine to validate me and what I knew in my heart to be my truth.

My truth may be different from your truth, and that's okay. I will ask you one thing – please believe in *something*. Believe that inside of you lives the same strength and energy that lives in me and your brothers and your sisters, connecting all of us in an unbelievable, yet undeniable, way.

What do you believe? Write it all down. Not what have you been told to believe, what you have been raised to believe, but what do you really believe in your heart to be true?

If your list mimics a certain religion, that is beautiful. If your list mimics no organized religion, that is beautiful. If the only word you wrote down was "love," that is beautiful.

Organized religions are not wrong if they ring true for you. If you feel nothing in your heart but love, if everything you feel about that religion is truth for you, then you are not living a lie. What is a lie is when you think your religion is the only one, the true and right religion that must and should be right for every single living soul on this earth. That isn't loving, that's arrogant.

Look past what organized religions have become – the books they gospel, the buildings they worship in, the laws they administer. Look back to the foundation of all religions. You will find love and only love. Forget all the lies and remember the only truth that matters – remember love.

I am lucky, I've never not believed in something. But I know plenty of people who don't believe in a divine being, God. Are they wrong? Of course not. I also know plenty of people who don't know *what* to believe. Are they wrong? Of course not. They just need to let go of the guilt or confusion they feel in order to be okay with not believing or not knowing.

For anyone who doesn't know, or simply says the divine is impossible, this bears repeating – at least believe in something. Believe in yourself. Believe that you have what it takes to win any battle, to turn unhappiness into joy, to be the best *you* that you can be. Believe that you can make a difference in your own life and the life of every single person you meet. Believe in love. Because when we believe in love, we create miracles.

Repeat this mantra all day today:
I believe.

I Can Make Miracles Happen

"Miracles occur naturally as expressions of love. The real miracle is the love that inspires them. In this sense everything that comes from love is a miracle."
— *A Course in Miracles*

What is a miracle? Jesus giving the blind man sight? A loved one beating cancer or another awful disease? Getting an "A" on an exam you thought you would fail? A rainbow? Yes, those are miracles. But miracles don't need to be extraordinary. In fact, the greatest miracles are simply ordinary.

I have used that word – "miracle" – many times throughout these pages. Miracles are something unexpected that love creates; answers that lie within you, not outside of you. We've learned together how choosing love creates miracles. You will see them now that you believe in them. The more you see them, the better your life will be.

When you choose love, miracles will occur. You will be grateful for every opportunity you have to change not only your day, but someone else's day as well. And without even realizing it, maybe even help change someone else's life.

Most people believe it would take a miracle to fulfill their dream. Simply choose love. Want to go on your dream vacation? The old you would have found excuses why you can't – you don't have the money and you don't have the time to take off from work. The new you puts twenty dollars a week aside instead of buying coffee and lunch out every day. The new you doesn't take unnecessary time off; you save your vacation days. Eventually, you realize that by choosing to love yourself enough to be deserving of this vacation, you now have enough money and time to fulfill your dream. You created a miracle.

You have just graduated from college with a degree in journalism but cannot find a job anywhere in your field. Instead of feeling defeated and questioning everything you've worked for, you start small – you blog about your journey on the job hunt. Next thing you know you are offered a small paycheck for your efforts. Miracle. You choose to love yourself enough to continue to move forward, to live what you love, no matter how small. I promise when you do this, when you choose love, your small steps forward will become as big as you allow them to.

After years of trying to make a difference, instead of giving in to the negative environment of your workplace, you realized it was hurting you more than you were helping others. You chose to walk away. You may never realize that it took your absence for your former co-workers to miss your kindness and begin expressing it themselves. People are a little nicer to each other, pay more attention, give a little bit more. These miracles didn't happen because you left, they happened because you were there in the first place. Sometimes we do not see the miracle we created. Some things we just have to take on faith.

You are a teacher who has spent unselfish time with your students. The quietest student, you don't even remember her name, becomes an inner-city teacher who helps students get into college who otherwise never would have. You may never know you were her inspiration. But by choosing to teach with love you created that miracle.

You are a fireman who rescued a child's cat from a tree. You never gave it a second thought, all in a day's work. That child, because you choose love, becomes a fireman a decade later and saves the life of woman trapped in her burning house. You created that miracle.

Always thinking positive, strong thoughts will create miracles. Walking without losing weight? Instead of gossiping or complaining to your co-worker during your walk, choose love and think about how strong you are becoming, how much more energy you are getting by moving every day. The weight will fall off. Are you always sick? Instead of being negative and waiting around for the next virus to find you, choose love and proactively take care of yourself. When you choose love you will heal quicker, get colds and flus less often.

Creating miracles needs to start somewhere. Why not here, now, with you? Choose to make miracles happen. Choose love. Show others how love can create miracles and change your life. Show others how simple life can be when you choose to ignore ego and listen to your inner voice and the laws of nature instead. Speak every word, extend kindness at every instance, knowing it will create a miracle. You will turn someone's sadness to joy, someone's anger to forgiveness, someone's confusion to understanding. See everyone and everything as a miracle. Show others that creating miracles is the way to peace.

Create miracles today. Do something kind – help a family member, a friend, or a stranger. Lead by example, show them the way it's done. Help them load groceries into their car or house. Rake their leaves, mow their lawn, shovel their snow. Donate your time to a good cause – money only goes so far, your*self* helps on every level and helps every*one*. Your *self* creates the miracle.

Repeat this mantra all day today:
I can make miracles happen.

I Am

"Before I can tell my life what I want to do with it,
I must listen to my life telling me who I am."
– Parker J. Palmer, *Let Your Life Speak*

Choosing love isn't just about finding peace for ourselves. It is also about leading the way so others can follow us there. We have gone from trying to doing. We view every "mistake" as an opportunity for correction and healing. We learn lessons and are ready to lead by example. We go from being a student to realizing that every situation is a chance to be both a student *and* a teacher.

Choosing love is more than talking the talk, it's walking the walk. It's loving without asking, "When is it my turn?" or, "Why haven't I gotten my reward yet?" When you are ready to realize that no one can fail – when you stop asking, "Why haven't they gotten this yet?" – you have gone from healing to healer.

During this journey to find peace, we learn about who we really are. And we realize that no amount of desire or prayer will simply give us what we want, we have to work for it! We have to practice and learn these new skills to find our way to peace. We have reached a higher understanding about ourselves and our place in this world, this universe, this life. Isn't it wonderful? *You* are wonderful! And now you finally believe it! Now it's time to take that new understanding about yourself to realize your life's purpose.

You started on this journey most likely because you are looking for a change. No matter what that change is you always know when that time for change has come. You feel it physically, mentally, and spiritually. Never be afraid. Follow your inner guidance and you will find your life's purpose.

Your inner guidance or gut instinct, the Holy Spirit, the Source – whatever you call it personally – has been guiding you through this journey from page one. It was that voice of awareness that had you pick up this book and say, "Yes! I'm ready!" That inner voice is the one telling you there is always a better way. Why not use that now to find the answer to the biggest question we all have – "Why am I here?"

Who do you want to be? What do you want to be? How do you want to be? Then BE IT! Get a clear picture of who you desire to be, and be who you want to be NOW! Go to bed every night as if you're already who you want to be. Think how a writer would think, feel how a romantic relationship would feel. Many mystics from Neville to Wayne Dyer call this I AM. In order to become who you want to be, you must imagine you are already that person. Feel it, think it, live it, become it. You have used this same principle to become the soul who is now looking for her life's purpose. Use this I AM principle now to finally find it.

"I want to be a writer." Then get off Facebook and Words with Friends once in a while and be a writer. Change your statement to, "I AM a writer."

"I want to find a lasting relationship." Then go to the movies, take yourself to dinner, buy yourself flowers. Do the things for and with yourself that you want to do with your future partner. Have a loving relationship with yourself and that love will find you. Change your statement to, "I AM love."

"I want a better job." Then take that class, enrich your skills, investigate the companies you're thinking about working for and start making contacts there. Change your statement to, "I AM in the best job for me."

What are you passionate about? What do you have enthusiasm for? Use that passion to give service to others. You have learned that by choosing love you create miracles. Choosing love always means doing for others, being generous, giving of ourselves for the benefit of someone else, and doing so without expectations. It's not about someone liking you or appreciating you. It's not about doing something nice for them so they will do something nice for you in return. To find your life's purpose you must do nice things for them because you *choose* to.

Know that just because you want something doesn't mean it's your calling. I can never be the ace pitcher for the Boston Red Sox no matter how much I wanted it when I was ten years old. When you really know you're in the right place, you don't call *it*, *it* calls you. Is what you want to do a struggle or do you do it effortlessly? Do you have to try or do you do it with ease? Do you need motivation? Do you let distractions get in your way?

Our life's purpose should be something we create in order to extend love to everyone and everything. What can you create? Simple. Create love. What do you love and how can you use it to serve others? Maybe it's gardening, the environment, children. Maybe it's simply people. Maybe it's not even about changing your entire life. Maybe it's about being the best *you* that you can be right exactly where you are right now. If all you are drawn to is sitting quietly, teach that, be that example. If you don't know what you're drawn to, retreat to the quiet and let your purpose find you.

Is your love for medicine or the holistic healing arts? Your love will create physical, emotional, and spiritual healing. Is your love for law enforcement or justice? Your love creates healing in the form of a safe society. Is your love for writing, drawing, painting, dancing, singing or playing music? Your love creates healing in the form of expression and emotion. Is your love for the environment? Your love will create healing for our earth, our bodies, and our communities.

Is your love for children? Maybe being a nurse isn't coming easy to you in the hospital. Turn your attention to what you love: children. Maybe you become a school nurse. Or maybe you realize nursing is just too hard after all and you realize you can love and help children even better by working in a daycare center. Do what you love and find a way to do it that comes easy for you.

Is your love for teaching? You do not have to be a teacher in a school to teach. How can you learn to teach today, right where you are? Can you teach your co-workers how to work more efficiently? Can you teach your children to choose love over hate? Even if you work at The Gap, become a teacher. Teach your customers and your coworkers. How? Choose love. Be kind, smile. Be your kindest to the angriest customer, be more positive than your disgruntled co-worker. Teach them about love and peace.

If you cannot leave your job, choose to stay where you are and teach others what it means to love. Be an example of love and that, in turn, creates healing for both yourself and everyone you serve. Choose to stay and, no matter what your job is, do it with love. Remember, you are there to be of service of others, not for your own egotistical gains. If you cannot do it with love, find a job you can. You're only hurting yourself and others by staying in a job you emotionally quit a long time ago. Find something you are passionate about, something where you can extend love and healing to yourself and others.

Know who you are. Know what your limitations are and what your strengths are. What miracles are you willing to create by choosing love over doubt or laziness? Know that where you are right now is perfect timing. You did not lose time. You are simply ready to move forward, right on time.

What did you like to create as a child? What hobbies did you have then that you still enjoy now? Did you like to draw, dance, color? Did you like to tinker with electronics, taking things apart and putting them back together? Did you like to play sports, put on plays, ride bicycles? Do it again today. How does it feel? How can you use this to find your life's purpose? Do it every day and your life's purpose will find you.

Do not wait for life to happen to you. Every step you take must be a step forward. You wrote a paragraph today, next week write two. You didn't get your dream job in New York? Then take that fitness instructor exam you've been thinking about taking. You are thinking about asking for your old job back? Don't. Find a different one, any one. Always move forward. Never look back.

Repeat this mantra all day today:
I AM.

Journey to Peace

"I'm not afraid... I was BORN for this!"
– Joan of Arc

When we journey through love to peace, we remember why we were created. Love is who we are on the inside and what we need to shine to the outside. Choosing love is about experiencing life with a smile and teaching the world how to heal. How do we know when we've made it?

When we are no longer afraid.

When we choose love, not anger.

When we compliment instead of complain.

When we hold our brother's hand instead of choosing to battle.

When we hug our sister not to console her during her turmoil, but because we no longer even see her wounds.

When we are healed and our world is healed.

When we realize we are not at the end, but at a new beginning.

When we remember that we are all on this journey to peace together...

When love wins.

About the Author

Tami Lee Hawley has been around books her entire life. She has worked in both traditional and college bookstores and as a librarian assistant at her local high school. She is certified in Advanced Reiki, an energy healing art.

Tami's maternal great great grandmother, Catherine Beggs Galvin, was a poet and school teacher in Ireland. Her great uncle, Catherine's son, Jimmy Galvin, was an editor at the Waterbury Republican-American newspaper. Her paternal grandfather, Manfred B. Lee (Manford Lepofsky), along with his cousin Frederic Dannay (Daniel Nathan), was the writing team that penned the Ellery Queen mystery novels. Writing is in her blood.

Tami lives in UConn country, Storrs, Connecticut, a mile from her alma mater, with her husband, Bob, and cats, Pokie and Blarney.

Tami can be reached through her website, TheDivineDove.com, where you can also purchase inspirational prints with quotes from this book. You can also receive guidance through Tami's messages as an Angel Card Reader. *When Love Wins: Our Journey to Peace* is her first book.

Acknowledgements

Thank you again to my mother, Arlene, for being my champion.

Thank you again to my husband, Bob, for being my best friend, my best editor, and my biggest fan.

Thank you to my late grandmother, Dottie, for telling me it was okay to always feel very deeply.

Thank you to my brother, Mike. I hope I can say I'm even half the writer you are.

To my brother, Dana, we may not always believe in the same things, but I thank you for always believing in me.

Thank you to my niece, Alexa, for our unbroken bond of love and affection.

Thank you to my niece and Goddaughter, Samantha, for the love and the hugs that have saved my life more than once.

Thank you to my Anam Cara, Colleen, for making me get up and dance again.

Thank you to my thicker-than-blood sister, Kathy, and to my Soul Sister, Jean, for taking this journey with me.

Thank you to Carol and Nancie. I wouldn't be here without either of you.

Thank you to Rebecca, Maika, Donna, Linda, Priscilla, and Heather for healing me and guiding me to places beyond my wildest dreams.

And to each one of you who found this book, I thank you. May you joyfully show others the way...

Peace and love to you all.